Jonah
His Life, Character, and Mission

PATRICK FAIRBAIRN

BAKER BOOK HOUSE
Grand Rapids, Michigan

Reprinted 1980 by
Baker Book House Company

ISBN: 0-8010-3498-1

First published in 1849

PHOTOLITHOPRINTED BY CUSHING - MALLOY, INC.
ANN ARBOR, MICHIGAN, UNITED STATES OF AMERICA

PREFACE

A PECULIAR and somewhat mournful interest
hangs around the life and labours of Jonah,
not surpassed, in some respects scarcely equal-
led, by that which attaches to any other of
the Old Testament prophets. The elements
both of evil and of good wrought with un-
wonted energy in his experience—at one time
depressing him to the lowest depths, and anon
raising him to a kind of supernatural elevation. Cast upon degenerate times, when the
foundations of the earth were out of course,
and the kingdom of God was, in a manner,
forced to strike out into new and unexpected
channels, it was his lot to tread strange and
mysterious paths—paths equally remarkable

for the sore troubles and the glorious achievements through which they conducted him—though himself meanwhile so ill prepared for the times, or the times so hardly set for him, that the bright, not less than the dark and cloudy, periods of his life served only to feed the well-spring of his sorrow and dejection.

Unhappy prophet! unhappy, too, in his posthumous connexion with the world, as well as in his personal sojourn in it; for the troublous spirit that attended him through life seems still to have slumbered in his ashes. Reproach and dishonour have been heaped upon his name amongst men. The adversaries of the truth, and not these only, but also its zealous friends and defenders, have shot many a bitter arrow at him, and have thought they improved the record of his singular history according as they enforced against him charges of transgression, and expressed their abhorrence of his character. Not so "the greater than he," whose servant and forerunner he was, and who once and again pointed an evil and adulterous genera-

tion to the wonderful experience and history
of Jonah as already containing the elements
of his own, and as pregnant with lessons of
highest wisdom to those among whom he lived.
And, following in his footsteps, we also have
sought to honour the son of Amittai, yea, to
vindicate his title to a distinguished place
among those who have done and suffered
much for the cause of God—men of noble
hearts and devoted lives—in whose very fail-
ings we still discern the lofty and self-denying
spirit that animated their bosom.

What we have written, however, in the following pages, is not to be regarded simply, nor
even chiefly, in the light of a vindication. The
aim rather has been to give a clear and just
representation of the times of the prophet—of
the nature and design of the singular mission
he was appointed to fulfil—and of the varied
instruction which is furnished for believers of
every age by the mission itself, and the manner
in which it was discharged. The work assigned this prophet marked in some respects
a new era in the providence of God toward his

Church; it unfolded principles of government
and ways of dealing, which again reappear in
other portions of prophetical scripture more
fully developed and variously applied; so that
the consideration of the book of Jonah, besides
the other advantages it yields, furnishes some
sure and well-defined landmarks for guiding
our way to a sound interpretation of the word
of prophecy. To sincere and earnest students
of that word the author presents this volume,
as a small contribution toward the right understanding of those portions of prophecy which
come within its range, and to all in general
who desire to cultivate an intimate acquaint-
ance with the records of God's revealed will.
May the Lord be pleased to accept the effort
here made to discover his truth, and manifest
his ways to the children of men!

CONTENTS

CHAPTER I

CHAPTER VII

CHAPTER VIII

CHAPTER IX

CHAPTER X

SUPPLEMENTARY REMARKS

PART I

PART II

PART III

JONAH

CHAPTER I

IT is always of importance for a correct understanding
of the prophetical scriptures, to know something of
the time when they were indited, and of the persons
to whom they were originally addressed. In the case
of Jonah it is not difficult to ascertain this, as a passage in the Second Book of Kings marks with sufficient distinctness the period of his agency in the affairs
of Israel. Speaking of the second Jeroboam, the
great-grandson of Jehu, and the last of his seed that
for any length of time occupied the throne of Israel,
the inspired historian says, " He restored the coast of
Israel, from the entering of Hamath unto the sea of
the plain, according to the word of the Lord God of
Israel, which he spake by the hand of his servant
Jonah, the son of Amittai, the prophet which was

of Gath-hepher (a town in the tribe of Zebulon); for
the Lord saw the affliction of Israel, that it was very
bitter; for there was not any shut up, nor any left,
nor any helper for Israel; and the Lord said not, that
he would blot out the name of Israel from under heaven, but he saved them by the hand of Jeroboam, the
son of Joash."—(2 Kings xiv. 25-27.)

This passage puts it beyond a doubt, that Jonah
was in the exercise of his prophetical office, certainly
not later than the commencement of the reign of
Jeroboam II.; for, the prediction he is recorded to
have uttered respecting the recovery of a part of the
Israelitish territory from the yoke of Syria was fulfilled by the hand of Jeroboam. And as this monarch, in fulfilling it, had to wage a difficult and
arduous warfare with Syria, in the course of which he
got possession of Damascus, the capital of the kingdom,
and raised Israel anew to much of its former splendour
and importance, we may certainly conclude, that he
was at the time in the vigour of his days, and that the
conquests achieved by his hand were made much
nearer the beginning than the close of his reign.
But the prophecy which foretold the result of these
conquests must have been earlier still. Nay, it was
manifestly uttered at a time when the affairs of Israel
were in the most shattered and depressed condition;
when, as it is said, "there was none shut up or left,"
that is, confined or left at large; when there was neither
bond nor free, the inhabitants of all conditions being
utterly wasted, and there seemed to be none that

could act the part of "a helper for Israel." But the kingdom of Israel was never in such a state at any period during the reign of Jeroboam, nor even when he ascended the throne. It had been so, indeed, in the days of his father Joash, who had found the kingdom reduced to the most abject subjection to the king of Syria; but he had gradually restored it, by a succession of victories, to comparative strength, and commenced the prosperous career which was only continued and carried out by Jeroboam. So that the utterance of Jonah's prediction concerning the recovery of Hamath and Damascus, seems rather to belong to the earlier part of the reign of Joash than to any period of Jeroboam's reign; and, though the fulfilment of it is ascribed only to Jeroboam, because it was he who recovered the more distant portion of the territory of which it spake, yet the prophecy itself appears to have equally included the preceding victories and nearer conquests of Joash.

We thus arrive at the result that Jonah was the earliest, in point of time, of all the prophets whose labours and predictions have been recorded in separate books. Hosea and Amos are both reported to have prophesied in the days of Jeroboam; but, from the other marks of time given in their writings, they could not have begun to prophesy till near the close of his reign.* The time of Jonah thus treads closely on

* Thus Amos expressly states, that he began to see his vision concerning Israel in the days of Uzziah and Jeroboam, two years before the earthquake. Now, this earthquake, we learn from

that of Elisha; and we can scarcely doubt that the
two were for some years contemporaneous.   Elisha
lived to an advanced age, and died some time in the
reign of Joash, before the close of his successful conflict
with the Syrians.   And, as Joash's entire reign did not
exceed sixteen years, we may reasonably infer that
Jonah, who in the course of that reign appeared on the
prophetic stage, had in his early years sat at the feet
of Elisha.   His first appearance also was of a kind
that fitly became the successor of that gentle and

Zech. xiv. 5, happened in the reign of Uzziah, king of Judah,
who did not begin to reign till about fourteen years before the
death of Jeroboam.   But Jeroboam reigned altogether forty-one
years, so that at whatever precise period in Uzziah's time the
earthquake may have happened, the two years before it, mentioned
by Amos as the commencement of his prophetical agency, necessarily carries us into the latter half of Jeroboam's reign.   Then
Hosea is said to have prophesied so late as the reign of Hezekiah,
king of Judah; and between even the last year of Jeroboam's
reign and the first of Hezekiah's, a period of about sixty years in-
tervenes.   He must, therefore, have been a very young man at the
close of Jeroboam's reign, and could not have entered on the
prophetic office much earlier.   So that Jonah, who seems to have
uttered a prediction in the days of Joash, was considerably
earlier than either of these prophets.   They were the next to
follow him; and as it is probable that the transactions recorded
in the book which bears his name took place in the latter period
of his life, the book itself may possibly not be much older than
some portions of the writings of Hosea and Amos.   Various reasons might be assigned for the Jews not placing his book precisely
at the commencement of the minor prophets; and the belief of
Lightfoot (*Chronica Temporum*) and many others, as to his being
actually later than Hosea and Amos, seems partly to have arisen
from a wrong view of his mission, of which afterwards.

humane ambassador of heaven; for the word then put into the mouth of Jonah, the only *direct* word, indeed, he is recorded to have uttered concerning Israel, was a word of mercy and consolation to the covenant people. It told them, that the Lord still yearned over them for their good, and would once more drive back the tide of evil which had been flowing in upon them, and recover the territory they had lost. Yet, while this promise of returning prosperity was held out, it was not doubtfully intimated, that all stood in an uncertain and hazardous position. The mercy of heaven hovered over the land, as if ready to take its departure; and the Lord had only *not said*, he would blot out the name of Israel, but neither had he said, he would preserve it. The fate of the kingdom hung in a kind of fearful suspense, as if He on whom its destinies depended, were waiting the issue of a last trial, to decide whether it was to be established in peace or given up to perdition.

Such was the posture of affairs in the kingdom of Israel when Jonah entered on his prophetical career. But whence originally arose this extreme danger? How did it happen, that, in a religious and moral point of view, they had come into so peculiarly critical and perilous a condition? It is necessary to know this, in order rightly to understand the future mission and history of the prophet of Gath-hepher; and it will consequently be proper here to take a rapid glance of the course which this kingdom of Israel had pursued since its commencement, and of the kind of deal-

ing to which it had been subjected on the part of
God.

The erection of the kingdom of Israel, or of the ten
tribes, into a distinct and separate government, it is
necessary to bear in mind, is constantly represented in
Scripture as a great evil. It came at the first as the visitation of a sore chastisement; and, so long as it existed,
it necessarily destroyed the unity of the covenant-people,
maintained a rival interest in what should have remained an undivided brotherhood of love, interfered
with the arrangement which conferred the rights of
royalty as a divine inheritance on the house of David,
and opened the door both for corruptions springing
up within, and for the assaults of adversaries making
havoc from without. Fraught as it necessarily was
with such great evils, the erection of the separate
kingdom could not fail to be displeasing to the mind
of God; nor could prosperity in the full sense—prosperity as designed and promised by God—be enjoyed
by either branch of the divided inheritance until the
breach was again healed, and the people were once
more united under one head of the house of David.
At the same time, there can be no doubt that, in a
certain modified sense, the erection of the separate
kingdom had God's sanction and approval. It came
expressly as a gift from God to Jeroboam, under the
hand of Ahijah the prophet, and with a promise from
the Lord, not indeed of its absolute perpetuity, but
of its prolonged existence, if Jeroboam and his seed
would walk in the ways of the Lord (1 Kings xi.

30–39). On this account, also, Rehoboam was discharged from attempting to reduce the lost tribes again under his dominion, as the Lord had meanwhile given them to Jeroboam. And for the reason of the proceeding, we must, no doubt, find it in the fact, that the house of David had proved unfit to exercise the high and responsible trust committed to it, as appointed to reign in God's name over God's heritage, and carry out the great ends of his spiritual and righteous government. The external power and glory that had come to be connected with the honour, was more than David's successors—more even than his most renowned and wisest successor—could properly bear and employ; even in his hands, it was abused to purposes of carnal pomp and selfish aggrandizement at home, and abroad to the rendering of Jehovah's name utterly distasteful, by the exaction upon the subject heathen of an oppressive tribute, and the enforcement of a galling yoke. Even the abominations of those surrounding heathen, which should have been striven against and dispelled by the manifestation of divine truth to their consciences, were taken by the house of David under its countenance and protection; and thus, instead of serving as a sacred lever to raise the state in all its relations into nearer contact with heaven, the elevation of that house was rather tending to depress it in condition and character to the level of an earthly kingdom. The Lord must, therefore, bring a shade over its external glory, and weaken the arm of its temporal power, in order, if possible, to check the carnalising tendency, and secure for it a higher good.

But the incompetency on the part of the house of David to bear the glory to which it had been exalted, had its counterpart among a large portion of the people, in their insensibility to the honour of having a visible representative of the most high God reigning over them, and their disposition to view the kingdom in the light of a mere human institution. Great pains had been taken by Samuel at the period of its institution to elevate the people's notions respecting it; and David, during his lifetime, had also exerted himself to the uttermost to give the kingly government a divine aspect in the eyes of the people, and awaken that higher and fuller development of the divine life, which it was the special calling of the Lord's anointed to foster and promote among the tribes of his inheritance. This David did partly by the vigour and righteousness of his administration, which ever had mainly at heart the interests of truth and piety; partly also by the new life and power which he infused into the tabernacle worship; and finally, by the composition and destination to public use of those divine songs, which were not more adapted to beget and nourish a spirit of devotion, than to identify in the minds of the people the peculiar glory of their nation with the royal dignity and blessed administration of David's house. Still, the people as a whole never became thoroughly adjusted to the constitution under which they were placed. They wanted spiritual discernment and faith to enter into the plan of God, and to realise their own honour in the honour of the house of David. A large proportion of them viewed its exaltation with a carnal and envious eye, and bore with impatience the yoke of its authority; for which, doubtless, the selfish and worldly spirit that so early appeared in that house itself furnished too ready an excuse. Therefore, on both accounts—both as a necessary chastisement and humiliation to the house of David, and as the most appropriate way of administering a wholesome discipline and instruction to the people—the Lord saw it needful to disturb and weaken the commonwealth for a time, by the erection within it of a separate kingdom. Happy if both parties had understood that this device was sanctioned only as a temporary expedient, a grievous evil in itself, though intended to work out an ultimate good, and an evil which, so long as it lasted, inevitably prevented the full inheritance of blessing which God had promised to bestow. This, however, they failed to do. The breach, instead of leading to true repentance for sin, and from that to mutual reconciliation on higher grounds, became perpetually wider and deeper. And those who attained to power in the new kingdom of Israel, were plainly bent on nothing more than on establishing their total independence of the house of David and the kingdom of Judah.

It was not against this, however, the *civil* aspect of the evil, that the prophets in the kingdom of Israel struggled, or were called directly to interfere. They

had to do only with the *religious* change, by which it
was soon followed, and which had in no respect the
sanction of God; but, on the contrary, his uncompromising resistance and severe reprobation. While
he in some sense authorized Jeroboam to erect the
ten tribes into a separate kingdom, he gave him no
permission to institute within its borders a separate
worship; and to throw, if possible, an effectual bar
against any attempt in that direction, he caused
Ahijah twice in the original message to Jeroboam, to
declare Jerusalem to be the one place he had chosen,
in which to put his name.—(1 Kings xi. 32, 36.)
Motives of worldly policy, however, induced Jeroboam
to disregard this plain intimation of the divine will,
and to set up a separate worship. For, he naturally
imagined, that if the people of his kingdom should
continue to go up to Jerusalem at the stated feasts,
their hearts in process of time would be won back to
the house of David, to the prejudice of his own
family, and the ultimate overthrow of his kingdom.
And so, pretending to a considerate regard for the
comfort and convenience of the people—that it was
too far for them to travel to Jerusalem—he consecrated two sanctuaries with their respective altars,
the one at Bethel in the south, the other at Dan in
the north. With these also he connected two golden
calves, which were apparently designed to hold the
same relative place to the sanctuaries at Dan and
Bethel, that the ark of the covenant did to the temple
at Jerusalem; were designed, in short, to serve (after

the manner of Egypt, where Jeroboam had spent many years of his life) as proper and becoming symbols of the true God. But such innovations were too palpably opposed to the law of Moses to meet with the approval of the priesthood; who therefore, with one consent, refused to enter the sanctuaries of Jeroboam, and minister at his altars. Their refusal, however, only led to another flagrant violation of the Mosaic constitution; for Jeroboam, still determined to adhere to his wretched policy, took and consecrated for priests of the vilest of the people—men needy in circumstances and worthless in character—entirely fitted to act the part of obsequious ministers to the royal will. Thus the religion introduced into the kingdom of Israel in four most essential particulars— its sanctuaries, altars, symbols of worship, and ministering priesthood—bore on it an earthly image and superscription, it was polluted at the centre by the inventions of men; and though most of the rites of Judaism were still retained in it, yet " the Lord could not smell in the solemn assemblies of the people, nor accept their offerings." Besides, the religion being thus essentially changed in character, it necessarily lost its moral influence on the people;— itself now a grovelling superstition, moulded after the will of man, and administered by unclean and servile hands, it could raise no effectual bulwark against the tide of human corruption; a rapid degeneracy ensued in the general character of the nation; and this again made way, as it proceeded, for further corruptions in

worship, until at last undisguised heathenism, with its
foul abominations and shameless profligacy of manners,
took possession of the field.*

Such were the inevitable results of the change introduced by Jeroboam into the worship of God,
which from being regarded as essential to the independence of the kingdom, was clung to ever afterwards with fatal obstinacy. But there were also
certain attendant circumstances which contributed
materially to accelerate the progress of the evil. Of
this nature was the secession of the Priests and
Levites, who went over in a body to the kingdom of
Judah—thus withdrawing from the kingdom of Israel
not a little of its spiritual life.—(2 Chron. xi. 13, 14.)
And not only did many in Israel continue as before

* The great evil of idolatry, even in its earliest and least offensive form—that is, when it does not set up a plurality of gods—
but only an image or symbol through which to worship the
supreme God, consists in its necessarily conveying low and de-
basing views of his character and glory. The mind contemplates
God through the symbol, and rests in the ideas it suggests.
Hence, as no symbol can adequately represent Jehovah, he can
never be known and worshipped as the true God where idolatry
is practised ; for example, the symbol of the bovine form, or
calf, as it is generally called in Scripture, was regarded in Egypt,
the country of its birth, as the emblem of productiveness; it represented God as the great producer, the source of all life and
sustenance, or material comfort.—(Wilkinson's Egypt, V. p. 194.)
And, no doubt, the promoters of the false worship in Israel
would endeavour to reconcile men to it, by asking if the representation it gave of God was not a just and honourable one? It
might have been such, indeed, if the God of Israel had been
merely the God of nature—the source of life and production as
these exist in the external world. But there is plainly nothing

to go up to Jerusalem to worship; but the growing evil in Israel on the one hand, and the revived zeal and prosperity of Judah and the house of David on the other, led multitudes to abandon altogether their inheritance in the kingdom of Israel, and go to reside in that of Judah.—(2 Chron. xv. 9.) Thus another large draft was made upon the life-blood of the nation. So strong was the tendency in this direction for some time in Israel, that we are told Baasha, the king of Israel, set about building Ramah as a convenient fortress for preventing the intercommunion between the two kingdoms.—(2 Chron. xvi. 1.) It appears afterwards, indeed, to have almost ceased; which is easily accounted for, as Judah itself became leavened with the surrounding corruption, and

moral, no germ of holiness in such an idea of God; it is just what all heathenism in some form or another always was, the deification of nature; whereas the true God is pre-eminently the Holy One and the Just; and precisely in proportion as this fundamental idea is lost sight of, in any form of religion, will its influence for good be found to decline, and the bonds of morality under it become loosened. From what has been said, it appears, and it is not unimportant to notice, that the worshipping of God anciently under the symbol of a calf, was relatively quite the same with acknowledging and worshipping him now simply as the God of nature. Those who disown or forsake God as he is revealed in the face of Jesus Christ, and who, neglecting his sanctuaries and his Sabbaths, go to explore him, as they say, in the works and operations of nature, are the legitimate followers of him who made Israel to sin. Worshippers of a shadow! their religion wants the reality of truth for its foundation, and being at best but a nature-worship, it has no moral power to regenerate and sanctify the heart.

alliances were even formed between the house of
David and the infamous family of Ahab, who carried
the apostasy to its height in Israel.

This second decline on the part of the house of
David and the kingdom of Judah, gave rise to a new
stage in the method of God's procedure toward Israel.
Hitherto he had left the testimony against the prevailing evil to be borne by the faithful still remaining
in the land of Israel, aided by the salutary influence
which had proceeded from Judah, and which was felt
even in some of the neighbouring heathen countries.
—(2 Chron. xv. 8, xvii. 9-11.)   When Judah, however, also began to prove unfaithful, and the iniquity
in Israel became more flagrant and atrocious, stronger
and more direct measures were required to meet the
evil.   These were found, first, in the gigantic energy
and labours of Elijah, who for a time fought single-
handed against the rampant idolatry; and then by
the new organization of the prophetic order, or the
re-establishment of the schools of the prophets, which
he accomplished with the aid of Elisha.   By these
means a very considerable revival was effected in the
kingdom of Israel, which reached even to the palace
of Samaria; for while Elijah, at the commencement
of his career, found it difficult to obtain standing-
ground for his ministry, the very name of Jehovah
being proscribed, there were, some time before his
death, four hundred prophets in Samaria who openly
professed to speak in the name of Jehovah.—(1 Kings
xxii. 5, 6.)   And a little further down in the history,

we find Joram, the son of Ahab, professing to entertain the highest respect for Elisha, and requesting Elisha's servant to rehearse the miraculous deeds that had been done by his hand.—(2 Kings iii. 12, viii. 4.)

But, whatever abatement this might indicate of avowed hostility against the worship and service of Jehovah, the original corruption remained in full vigour; and it would even seem, that, under a certain disguise, the worship and service of Baal held its place to the last. For though, on the occasion of Ahab's going up with Jehoshaphat to Ramoth-Gilead, the prophets all professed to speak in the name of Jehovah, yet there was evidently a marked contrast between the four hundred who had the confidence of Ahab, and Micaiah, who alone uttered the mind of the Lord. And on another occasion, when Jehoshaphat and Joram were engaged in the war with Moab, and they went together to ask counsel of Elisha, the prophet indignantly addressed the king of Israel with the words: "What have I to do with thee? Get thee to the prophets of thy father, and to the prophets of thy mother;"—plainly indicating that these still were virtually prophets of Baal. Not only so, but when Jehu was executing his fearful commission against the house of Ahab, a false proclamation brought out four hundred in Samaria—an ominous number, being precisely that of those who had formerly contended with Elijah on Carmel, and were slain—who styled themselves prophets of Baal, and as such were put to death.—(2 Kings x.) And passing a few generations more, as we approach the close of the kingdom of Israel, we find the worship of Baal again rising into notice as part of the prevailing abominations for which the wrath was made to fall upon them to the uttermost : " And they left all the commandments of the Lord their God, and made them molten images, even two calves, and made a grove, and worshipped all the host of heaven, and served Baal."—(2 Kings xvii. 16.) To which may be added the testimony of Hosea ii. 13 : " And I will visit upon her the days of Baalim, wherein she burned incense to them, and she decked herself with her earrings and her jewels, and she went after her lovers, and forgat me, saith the Lord."—(See also Micah vi. 16.)

It would seem therefore, that with the mass of the people, and in the high places of the land, there had been only a superficial improvement, but no thorough reformation. The terrible displays which Jehovah had given of his power and glory, and especially the slaughter of Baal's prophets on Mount Carmel, had inspired the worshippers of that Syrian deity with terror ; and afraid of again provoking such awful outbursts of judgment, but still unwilling to abandon their corruptions, they attempted to compound the matter by calling Baal Jehovah, and Jehovah Baal,—(hence, " Thou shalt call me no more Baali," my Baal, Hosea ii. 16),—as if these were but different names for one and the same God. This was in the highest degree insulting to Jehovah, because, in the most offensive manner, it lifted up his name to a thing of vanity, and proceeded on the supposition that there was no fundamental difference between him and the idol gods of the Gentiles. And that the people at large, in particular the more wealthy and influential classes, really viewed the object of their worship rather as an impure Syrian deity than the heart-searching righteous Jehovah, is abundantly manifest from those portions of the prophetical writings which describe the moral condition of Israel in the last years of their political existence, and which represent the land as all polluted with scenes of lust, revelry, oppression, rapacity, and crime.—(See especially Amos ii. 6-8; v. 7-15; vi.; Hos. iv.; Isa. v.; ix. 8-21.)

To sum up the whole. The grand evil in the kingdom of Israel was the idolatry and corruption introduced into God's worship, with its natural and necessary consequences. The Lord in various ways caused a solemn protest to be lifted against the evil at the period of its introduction—by the self-denying resistance of the priests and Levites—by the warning voice of the prophet that went from Judah (1 Kings xiii.), and the appalling word of judgment delivered by the aged Abijah to Jeroboam's wife (1 Kings xiv. 9–11). The protest was for some time vigorously maintained by a faithful remnant in the kingdom, who refused to assemble for worship at Dan and Bethel, but still repaired to Jerusalem, and not a few of whom ultimately went to settle there. It was further maintained, or rather in another and more

palpable form raised by Elijah and Elisha, and the
schools of the prophets instituted by them, who
formed a kind of supernatural order of God's servants
in the kingdom, called forth by the emergency of the
times—a provisional substitute for the exiled priesthood of the house of Aaron—and a standing witness
against the existing worship, from whose unauthorized
priesthood and disallowed services they stood entirely
aloof. By terrible things in righteousness the Lord had
also protested against the evil, having expressly on this
ground first cut off the house of Jeroboam, then the
house of Baasha, then Zimri, then the family of
Ahab—while, at the same time, he raised up the
kingdom of Syria as an instrument of evil to scourge
and afflict the land of Israel in its borders. And
now, at the time of Jonah's appearance on the stage
of history, the house of Jehu, because they also followed in the same forbidden course, had been brought
to the verge of ruin, and the whole kingdom lay
bleeding under strokes of judgment so severe, that
recovery seemed almost hopeless. But divine compassion was not yet exhausted, the Lord remembered
once more his covenant, and, seeking to win the people
again to his love and service, he gave yet another promise of returning prosperity, which he also fulfilled
by the hands of Joash and Jeroboam. This new
course of prosperity, however, only supplied new wings
to corruption ; a more heedless infatuation and widespread profligacy every where appeared ; and, sinking
into profound carnality of spirit, the people had come

to ascribe both their former troubles and their present prosperity to merely natural causes, "not regarding the works of the Lord or the operation of his hands." But might there still not be another, if possibly a final and desperate, effort put forth for their recovery? One that, from its very nature, might at once bespeak the inexcusable nature of their impenitence, and the certainty, if continued, of immediate retribution? There *was* such another, and we find it in the great work and mission of Jonah. Though bearing respect immediately to the Ninevites, it spoke also in the loudest and most impressive manner to the people of Israel, and was even like the shooting of God's last arrow of mercy, leaving no alternative in respect to them, should it prove ineffectual, but the speedy execution of vengeance.

CHAPTER II

JONAH, we have already seen, was a prophet in the
kingdom of Israel; and as the prophetical gift, like
every other communication of the Spirit, was always
bestowed for the special benefit of the visible church,
we cannot doubt, that to be a witness to Israel was
the great end and object of his mission.   But the
singular thing is, that when we turn to the Book of
Jonah, which contains the record of his prophetical
calling, we find no mention whatever made of Israel;
the commission given him calls him away to another
land, and requires him to transact with the inhabitants of a heathen city.   The word that came to him
was, "Arise, go to Nineveh, that great city, and cry
against it; for their wickedness is come up before
me."   The message, too, with which he was charged,
appears in the circumstances scarcely less strange in
regard to its matter, than in regard to the people to
whom it was to be delivered.   It was to be simply a
cry against their heaven-daring iniquities, and an
intimation that God was ready to come down to the

execution of judgment. But why send such a message to Nineveh by this prophet, when there was so loud a call for it at home? The people of Israel, his own kinsmen, had now also reached a condition of almost hopeless profligacy and corruption; so that the cry of *their* iniquity must still more have gone up to the heavens, and called for the summary execution of divine wrath. Nor can we reasonably doubt, though the fact is not expressly recorded, that this prophet, after the example of those who preceded him in Israel, took many occasions in the course of his ministry to reprove the evil of the times, and to proclaim the certain approach of judgment. Yet it can as little be doubted, on the other hand, that the special work he had to do as a witness of heaven against the abounding iniquity, and a sign to Israel of the mind of God respecting it, consisted in the work committed to him as God's ambassador to a people who lay altogether beyond the territory of Israel, and who had not hitherto been subjected to any peculiar moral treatment.

The appearance of strangeness, however, which this at first sight presents, will be found to vanish when the whole circumstances of the case are taken into consideration, and the bearing is seen which the singular work now to be wrought by God was designed and naturally fitted to have upon Israel. Why Nineveh in particular should have been chosen as the theatre of such an experiment—for this, indeed, we have no definite reason to assign beside the sovereignty of God; as there were, no doubt, many other cities at that time to which a similar message might with equal propriety have been sent. But there were two properties in the condition of Nineveh which rendered it peculiarly suitable for the great object contemplated by God; these were the magnitude of its population and resources, and the enormity of its crimes. In the word to Jonah, it is simply styled " that great city" (literally, " a great city of God"), an appellation which seems also to have been in familiar use among heathen writers. By these the most extraordinary accounts have been handed down of its grandeur and extent; it is even reported to have been " much greater than Babylon," and to have been surrounded with walls " a hundred feet high, and so broad that three waggons might be driven on them abreast." These walls, we are further informed, were fortified with 1500 towers at proper distances, each rising 200 feet in height, and rendering the whole so strong that the city was thought to be impregnable. That it should, therefore, have contained 120,000 little children, as we learn from the last chapter of Jonah, or an entire population approaching to a million, need not at all surprise us. It is also in perfect accordance with those other accounts derived from heathen sources, to have it spoken of as a city of three days' journey; taking this in connection with the twofold fact, that a day's journey in so hot a climate necessarily indicates a much shorter space than it does here, and that the cities of the East in ancient times comprehended in their circuit, as they often do still, many gardens and large spaces of vacant ground. Finally, being situated on the banks of the Tigris, and occupying a position most convenient for an emporium of merchandise between Eastern and Western Asia, we are quite able to understand how such a magnificent city should have arisen there, and how the prophet Nahum should speak of her as having "multiplied her merchants above the stars of heaven," and as revelling in wealth and luxury.*

Considering the immense greatness which ancient Nineveh is thus known to have attained, and perceiving how large and populous cities invariably become nurseries of vice and corruption, it is precisely what we might have expected to learn, that the wickedness of Nineveh kept pace with its commercial

* We have the fullest confirmation of the ancient accounts respecting Nineveh, in the recent elaborate and beautiful work of Mr Layard on Nineveh, and its remains: "The city had now attained the dimensions assigned to it in the book of Jonah, and by Diodorus Siculus. If we take the four great mounds of Nimroud, Kouyunjik, Khorsabad, and Karamles, as the corners of a square, it will be found that its four sides correspond pretty accurately with the 480 stadia, or 60 miles of the geographer." He here mentions in a note, that "from the northern extremity of Kouyunjik to Nimroud is about 18 miles; the distance from Nimroud to Karamles, about 12; the opposite sides of the square, the same. Twenty miles is the day's journey in the East; and we have consequently the three days' journey of Jonah for the circumference of the city. The agreement of these measurements is remarkable." "Within the space there are many large mounds, including the principal ruins in Assyria, and the face of the country is strewed with the remains of pottery, bricks, and

importance and external greatness. The language
used respecting it to Jonah, is quite similar to that
employed at an earlier period concerning Sodom and
Gomorrah, and denotes a state of flagrant immorality
and vicious abandonment. They were no ordinary
iniquities that were proceeding in the midst of it, but
such as raised a cry that pierced the very heavens, and
would no longer permit the righteous God, whose ears it
entered, to look on as a silent spectator of the evil.

To send a messenger of heaven to such a city with
a word of solemn rebuke and warning, supposing the
mission not to be in vain, was a proceeding so unusual
in its nature, and of so public a character, that it was
evidently intended, as well as peculiarly fitted, to
arrest the attention of others besides those whom it
more immediately concerned. The pre-eminent great-

other fragments. The space between the great public edifices was
probably occupied by private houses, standing in the midst of
gardens, and built at distances from one another, or forming
streets, which enclosed gardens of considerable extent, and even
arable land. The absence of the remains of such buildings may
easily be accounted for. . . . . . There is, however, sufficient to
indicate, that buildings were once spread over the space above
described; for, besides the vast number of small mounds every
where visible, scarcely a husbandman drives his plough over the
soil without exposing the vestiges of former habitations. Existing ruins thus show, that Nineveh acquired its greatest extent
in the time of the kings of the second dynasty; that is to say of
the kings mentioned in Scripture. It was then that Jonah visited
it, and the reports of its size and magnificence were carried to
the West, and gave rise to the traditions, from which the Greek
authors mainly derived the information handed down to us."—
Vol. ii. pp. 247–249.

ness of the city, with its wide-spreading commerce and its unrivalled splendour, rendered it more than any other place, in that region of the world, a city set upon a hill; so that, whatever extraordinary result might be achieved there, it could not be as a thing done in a corner, but must send forth its report, as from a public theatre, to the nations around. Then its crying sins and abominations, while they rendered it peculiarly obnoxious to the condemnation of heaven, being found in connection with such gigantic strength and manifold resources, seemed to bid defiance to any attempt at reformation. Who could have ventured to predict on any grounds open to human calculation, that a city, at once so immersed in sin and so richly furnished with the means of security and defence, would quail before the voice of a single preacher of repentance, and that too the voice of a stranger? But if this one call to repentance, notwithstanding the unlikelihood of its success, should still prove effectual—if the prophet of Israel, after having so long laboured in vain among his own people, should, by a kind of stray effort in the streets of Nineveh, become first the reformer and then the saviour of a mighty nation, what a loud rebuke and what a solemn warning should the whole transaction administer to backsliding and impenitent Israel!—a people who had been long dealt with by special ambassadors of God, among whom an entire order of prophets for successive generations had been plying their high vocation; while yet no successful inroad had been made on the prevailing idolatry and corruption! Would it not seem as if God were acting toward them as the parent who, wearied with the long-continued and obstinate waywardness of a son, and now almost despairing of his recovery, should try once more to work upon the heart of the hardened profligate, by turning aside for a little to address himself to some wandering and neglected outcast? And, having found this wretched and homeless stranger ready to listen to the first word of wholesome counsel and rebuke, should then make his appeal to the home-born child by holding up the instructive example furnished by the other? " Does not the sight of this reclaimed outcast, so soon reclaimed, at length make thee ashamed of thy perverse and foolish behaviour? Wilt thou still stand out, as thou hast hitherto done, against a father's advice and entreaty? What, then, can I do to thee more? What *should* I do, but henceforth leave *thee* to the fate of an outcast, no longer worthy to be called a child, and honour this recovered alien above thee, to thy perpetual shame and confusion?"

Such precisely, it will be remembered, was the use which our Lord made of the preaching of Jonah at Nineveh, and the success that attended it. He told the men of his own generation, among whom he had gone preaching the things of God's kingdom, that the people of Nineveh would rise up in the judgment to condemn them, because *they* had repented at Jonah's preaching; while He, a greater than Jonah, spoke only to cold and unconcerned hearts. But for the men who lived in the days of Jonah himself, the lesson came still closer; and the inference could scarcely fail to force itself on all but the most senseless and brutish minds, that the Lord, perceiving the hopelessness of any direct efforts, was now seeking to provoke his people to jealousy by the fruitful example of the Ninevites, and, at the same time, to press on their notice the imminent perils that surrounded their condition. Indeed, the procedure in respect to Nineveh was just an embodying of the principle so long before announced by Moses: "They have moved me to jealousy with that which is no god; they have provoked me to anger with their vanities: and I will move them to jealousy with those which are not a people; I will provoke them to anger with a foolish nation." See Nineveh, he in a manner exclaimed, that hitherto no people of mine, that foolish nation, how they have bowed their hearts at my call, and broken off their sins by repentance at the first intimation of my threatened judgments; while you, my covenant-people, the children of my kingdom, have only despised my words, and hardened your hearts against my fear! How can I longer delay to vindicate my righteousness in your destruction? And if, in proceeding to do this, I should give to these penitent strangers the ascendancy over you, and honour them as the rod of mine anger to chastise your backslidings, must not your own hearts discern the justice of the retribution?

This principle, from its very nature, could not possess a merely local or temporary place in the divine government, but is common to all ages. Accordingly, we find it again re-appearing at the beginning of the gospel, and even brought prominently into notice both in the words and the actions of our Lord. Not only did he make the appeal already mentioned, from the heedless and hardened impenitence around him, to the Ninevites under the preaching of Jonah; but when the centurion, a native heathen, came beseeching the interposition of his healing power in behalf of a dying servant, and giving utterance to a strength of faith at which Jesus himself is said to have marvelled, our Lord seized the opportunity to declare, that this example of faith from a Gentile far surpassed what he had yet found in Israel; that many like examples of faith, however, were soon to arise among the different nations of the earth, who would thus attain to the heritage of Abraham, while the children of the kingdom, from the want of it, should go into perdition. "Verily, I say unto you, I have not found so great faith, no, not in Israel. And I say unto you, That many shall come from the east and west, and shall sit down with Abraham, and Isaac, and Jacob, in the kingdom of God. But the children of the kingdom shall be cast into outer darkness: there shall be weeping and gnashing of teeth."—(Matt. viii. 11–12.) Various parables, also, were spoken by our Lord, for the purpose chiefly of enforcing the same lesson; in particular, that of the royal marriage (Matt. xxii. 1-14), and the parable of the wicked husbandmen (Matt. xxi. 33-41), which was concluded by so direct and pointed an appeal to the Jewish hearers, as to leave no room to doubt regarding the contemplated change: "Therefore say I unto you, The kingdom of God shall be taken from you, and given to a nation bringing forth the fruits thereof." This threatened expulsion of the Jews from the kingdom not only soon passed into a reality, but the footsteps of the divine procedure in accomplishing it followed exactly the same course as they had done in the days of Jonah. Grieved as the Lord now was with the wicked behaviour of the Jews, who even exceeded the measure of their fathers, he did not at once cast them off; but endeavoured, in the first instance, to shame them into repentance and amendment of life, as well as to warn them of impending danger, by presenting to their view all around them multitudes of converted heathens—persons who had once been wretched and depraved idolaters, but who had now become, through the gospel of his salvation, enlightened and spiritual believers. Had the eyes of the Jewish people not been utterly blinded, and themselves given up to a reprobate mind, they would have found in this, God's last and loudest call to repentance, the final movements of the kingdom as regarded them, preparatory to its complete departure. But, instead of viewing the divine procedure in this light, their minds were only inflamed by it to a more bitter and settled enmity against the truth of God. The warnings of the past and the les-

sons of the present were alike lost upon them; and
no alternative remained, but to take from them the
appearance of what they had already ceased to possess,
the reality—to put an end, by an outward change in
their condition, to their formal relation to God, and
send them forth into the world with the brand of aliens
and outcasts.

The same principle, we need scarcely say, is often
acted upon still, as well in regard to single individuals
as to entire communities, by the removal of the
candlestick out of its place, when the light has come
to be neglected and despised, and the exaltation of
the least favoured with outward privilege, over such
as have been most favoured, to the peculiar blessings
of the kingdom. This, however, has so often been
made matter of illustration and remark, that we have
no intention to dwell on it at present; but would
rather draw attention to the important and fundamental truth—too much lost sight of by the greater part
of those who handle the affairs of ancient Israel—on
which the method of procedure now in question is
based. That truth is, that God is not, neither was
formerly any more than now, a respecter of persons;
and that, when he chose the seed of Abraham and
endowed them with peculiar promises of blessing, the
objects of his regard and blessing were not simply the
offspring of Abraham, but that portion of them who
possessed his spirit of faith and obedience—his natural spiritual seed. This truth arises from the nature
of God as the righteous and unchangeable Jehovah—

every where and perpetually the same; so that he cannot be to one what he is not ready to be to another in like circumstances; and what manifestations he gives of himself in one place, or in one age of the world, these he is in substance constantly repeating in others. The revelation he gave of himself to Abraham speaks substantially the same language to all, even to the end of time and in the remotest corners of the earth, who occupy the same spiritual relation with the patriarch, but contains no assurance of blessing to persons differently related, not though they might be able to trace with the utmost certainty their descent from the loins of Abraham; for the personal relation being different, the nature of God's manifestation can no longer be the same.

Now, the Israelites were in peculiar danger of forgetting this truth, after having received so much as a people of the promised goodness of God, and finding themselves securely settled in the land of Canaan. It then became one of their strongest temptations, and, as the event proved, their capital error, to conclude that natural descent from Abraham was all that was necessary to constitute their title to the inheritance they enjoyed; and that God was, in a manner, so pledged to them, his word of promise so bound up with their experience of good, that they could not, without dishonour to his faithfulness, be dispossessed of their territory, and supplanted by men of another nation. The right by which they thus sought to hold the land, and the general promise of blessing, was thrown upon a merely natural ground, which being for ever fixed and settled in the past, could not, they imagined, be materially affected by any thing that might take place in the future; their calling was a concluded transaction, and, happen what may, they must still be the chosen of God, and all besides outcasts and aliens.

There could not be a more fatal error; for as in God's character the moral element ever holds the highest place, so must it always come most prominently out in his dealings toward his people; all must be subservient to the claims and interests of holiness. Therefore, foreseeing the danger to which Israel would be exposed in this respect, the Lord took every precaution from the first to prevent the error referred to from taking root among them. He made it clear as noonday to every spiritual eye, at the very commencement of their history, that while the promise was to run in the line of Abraham's posterity, yet not there indiscriminately, only in so far as they breathed his spirit and trod in his footsteps. Hence the successive limitations in the seed of Abraham, as connected with the promise: not Ishmael, as being merely a child of nature, born after the flesh, but Isaac, the special gift of God; again, not Esau, the man of natural impulse and pleasure, but Jacob, the man of faith. These successive limitations manifestly did not happen at random—they were a revelation from God, to make plain to future times whom in these covenant transactions he understood by the seed of blessing, namely, the natural-spiritual offspring of Abraham ; so that, if the natural only existed, the peculiar or covenant blessing failed. It was scarcely possible, indeed, for the distinction to be kept up so plainly afterwards, when the descendants of Jacob were formed into a nation, and when many, who were simply connected with him by natural descent, came unavoidably to be mixed up with those who were also spiritually his children. But it was evident, from what had been done at the commencement, that the distinction would still be kept up in the view of God. And not only so, but to render the distinction as far as possible manifest to the eye of sense—to show that they only who were Israelites indeed were entitled to an Israelite's name and inheritance—and that if any others shared in the things outwardly belonging to it, it was from no title conferred on the part of God, but only from the faulty and imperfect administration of his will on the part of man:—with this view more immediately the law entered before the people were permitted to take possession of Canaan, and was formed, along with the original promise to Abraham, into a covenant engagement between them and God ; so that, while the one presented them with a title to the inheritance, the other furnished them with a criterion for determining whether the title were actually theirs. For, given as the law was, in what light could its requirements of holiness be regarded, but as a representation of the character of those whom God owned to be the rightful inheritors of the land—

the Jacob, as they are called in the 24th Psalm, or
the generation of pious worshippers, whom alone
God recognized as the seed of Jacob? And when,
along with this law of holiness, the Lord coupled
the stern injunction, so often repeated, that such
as wilfully transgressed them were to be cut off
from among their people, what could more clearly
indicate that he considered all such as properly aliens
—false children, on whom he had settled no dowery
of blessing? *

It is on this ground that the Psalmist David so
often identifies his personal enemies—who were enemies to him only because he represented the cause of
God—with the heathen or aliens. He could not regard them as properly belonging to the seed of Jacob,
or occupying any other relation than that substantially of the uncircumcised. Thus, in Ps. lix., written
on the occasion of Saul's party watching David in the

* The injunction about cutting off transgressors from among the
people of God, has often been referred to as a proof of the harsh
spirit of Judaism—but quite falsely. It was an essential part of
the Mosaic legislation; for the whole of this was constructed on
the principle of its having to do with the true people of God, the
seed of blessing, with the view of securing the continuance of
such a seed, and their inheritance of the blessing. The land in
which they were established was the Lord's land—the people,
therefore, must be his people, in character as well as name, and
the ordinances adapted to persons in such a condition. Otherwise, the whole would necessarily have given a wrong impression
of God, and conveyed a false instruction. Wilful transgressors
were, *ipso facto*, cut off from the covenant, and should have been
formally excluded or destroyed by the Church, just as now open
sinners should be excommunicated, and must finally be destroyed.

house with the design of killing him, he says of those merely domestic enemies : " They run and prepare themselves without my fault : awake to help me, and behold. Thou therefore, O Lord God of hosts, the God of Israel, awake to visit all the heathen : be not merciful to any wicked transgressors." " Swords are in their lips ; for who (say they) doth hear ? But thou, O Lord, shalt laugh at them ; thou shalt have all the heathen in derision."—(See also Ps. ix. 5, 15 ; x. 16 ; cii. 8 ; cxliv. 11.)   And in like manner, when the people generally had become children of disobedience, as unquestionably was the case in the kingdom of Israel when Jonah lived, the Lord gave them distinctly to understand, that he disowned them as that seed of Abraham to whom he had given by a covenant engagement the inheritance of the land of Canaan, and that they were now related to him much as the surrounding heathen.   The mission itself of Jonah to Nineveh virtually declared as much ; for it obviously implied, that a heathen city afforded now as legitimate a field for the labours of an Israelitish prophet as the kingdom of Israel, while the result proved it to be a much more propitious soil.   But what was only implied in this transaction was soon afterwards broadly announced by the prophet Amos, in the following cutting interrogations : " Are ye not as children of the Ethiopians unto me, O children of Israel ? saith the Lord.   Have not I brought up Israel out of the land of Egypt ? and the Philistines from Caphtor ? and the Syrians from Kir ?"   The

one precisely as the other; you stand, as the present possessors of Canaan, exactly on a footing with
those other nations in regard to their existing settle-
ments; no more in your case than in theirs do the
territorial changes that have taken place prove your
connexion with the everlasting covenant of God;
all is reduced now to the natural; the spiritual
relation, and with that the title to the blessing,
is gone.

It is of great importance to bear in mind this principle, which runs like a sacred thread through all
God's transactions with his ancient people, whether
these transactions be viewed more directly in the
bearing they have upon the natural descendants of
Abraham, or more indirectly upon the world at large.
In the former point of view, it shows, that while God
for certain wise and important reasons, which had respect to the good of others as well as their own,
chose Abraham and his offspring in a certain line to
the enjoyment of peculiar privileges, there was nothing
in his method of procedure arbitrary or capricious.
He did not act as if determined to bless them, simply
because they belonged to a particular race, and could
trace their descent from the father of the faithful.
St Peter announced no new principle in the house of
Cornelius, when he said, " Of a truth I perceive that
God is no respecter of persons;" but an old principle,
on which God had acted toward Israel itself through
all the history of the past, though Peter, like most of
his countrymen, had been so blinded by prejudice as

to have failed hitherto to perceive it. In the calling of Israel as a people, indeed, there was distinguishing grace, singling them out from the mass of the world to the enjoyment of peculiar advantages, but still no blind favouritism or foolish partiality; for the children of privilege could become the heirs of blessing only by yielding themselves as a spiritual seed to the Lord, and, if they failed in this, they entailed upon themselves a heavier doom. In a word, Canaan as a token of the divine favour and an inheritance of blessing, was the gift of Heaven *only to believing and spiritual men;* and, in so far as persons of a different description partook with them of the outward boon, it was only as the mixed multitude that followed Israel out of Egypt; they were there by sufferance only, and not by right or as proper denizens of the kingdom of God. It is only by keeping this in mind, that we can properly understand the nature of God's covenant relation to the seed of Abraham, and see how, amid outward failures, he was still faithful to his promises.*

---

* The principle which we have just unfolded is in one particular aspect brought very prominently out by the apostle Paul in his Epistle to the Romans, viz., in reference to the blessing of justification, which belonged to Abraham and to his seed only as standing in faith; and it is by keeping clearly in view the principle itself, that we can properly understand and account for some of the expressions used, and especially those in chap. iii. 30: " Seeing it is one God that shall justify the circumcision by (ἐκ) faith, and uncircumcision through (διὰ) faith." The peculiarity here lies in the use of the two prepositions, which the commen-

It is necessary to add, however, that what has now
been stated respecting the covenant of God, applies
to it only in so far as it came into contact with man's
responsibilities and obligations of duty, not in its

tators regard as synonymous; "and yet," as Tholuck justly
remarks, "the change can scarcely be thought to have been
undesigned." When he adds, however, that "perhaps it im-
plies a gentle stroke of irony, of which we have elsewhere in St
Paul's writings still stronger examples," he only shows how
little he was able to find his way to the true solution. To come
at this, we must bear in mind two things: first, that the apostle
has in his eye an essential distinction between the circumcised
and the uncircumcised, there having been all along a justified
portion among the one, but not among the other; and then, that
the justified among the circumcised were not all who possessed
the outward sign—not the circumcision *per se*, but the circumcision who had faith. If we bear these things in mind, we shall
easily perceive that there was an occasion for using different prepositions, and that the two actually employed are used in their
proper and distinctive import. The preposition ἐκ, says Winer,
with his usual accuracy, "is originally used in reference to such
objects as come forth out of the interior of another, *from within;*
and, transferred to internal relations, it denotes every source and
cause out of which something emanates."—(*Gram.*, p. 296, 297.)
Now, it is precisely in this general sense, as denoting the relation *from*, or *out of*, that the preposition is used by the apostle in
the passage before us. He is setting forth the identity in principle of God's method of justifying the saved, as well among
Jews as Gentiles: he is "the same God,"—the sameness of his
procedure in the two cases *proves* him to be the same. For, in
justifying the circumcision, it is not the circumcision as such, or
all indiscriminately who belong to it, but only "the circumcision
of (not *by*) faith;" that is, expressing the matter more fully, he
justifies simply that portion of the circumcised who have their
standing in faith, and out of that, as the ground of their spiritual
being, have received the sign of circumcision. So also in justi-

higher connexion with the ultimate designs and purposes of God. In this respect the covenant, standing
simply in the sovereignty and power of divine grace,
did infallibly secure a seed of blessing out of the natural posterity of Abraham, which was preserved through

fying the uncircumcision, it is done "*through* faith,"—through
this as the means of their entering into substantially the same
condition as was possessed by the true or spiritual circumcision.
The uncircumcised, as such, did not stand in faith; nor did they
possess the privilege of a justified condition; they needed to be
brought into this as a new state, and it was *through faith* that
the transition could alone be made. The circumcised, on the
other hand, were already in a justified state—if only their circumcision stood in faith, as the ground or root out of which it
came. So that the prepositions are each used in their proper
meaning, and there is by no means, as is commonly alleged, a
distinction without a difference. The statement simply is: The
circumcised out of faith (as contradistinguished from those who
are circumcised without faith) are justified; and so also are the
uncircumcised, who through faith enter into the same spiritual
condition. And the apostle then goes on to show, in chap. iv.,
how, in the case of the circumcised, it was not their being the
circumcision alone, but their being the circumcision of faith,
which secured their being in the condition of the justified. The
other passages, where ἐκ πίστεως, and also ἐξ ἔργων, are used in
connexion with justification—(for example, Rom. i. 17, iii. 20;
Gal. ii. 16, &c.)—are all to be interpreted in the same manner as
above. The expressions are never synonymous, though constantly
regarded so by commentators, with διὰ πίστεως, διὰ ἔργων; but
always point to the ground, or standing-point, out of which the
individual is contemplated. Justification or salvation is of faith,
not of works; the one is, the other is not, the condition out of
which the benefit comes to the possession of the soul. Of course,
if we look only to the general meaning, it is not materially different to say, that salvation is *through* faith, not through works,
as the means of its attainment.

all backslidings and corruptions till the covenant was
for ever ratified and made sure in Christ. And it
seems to be implied in the reasoning of the apostle
(Rom. xi. 25-32), that the grace of the covenant
would still be continually securing an election from
the natural seed, till the whole should be brought to
a participation in the blessing. But of this only by
the way.

The principle, however, on which God's covenant
with Abraham was founded and administered, as now
represented, is not less important when viewed in respect to the world at large. For, the spiritual seed
being throughout alone the seed of blessing, the spiritual element was thus clearly elevated above the
natural, and determined to be the real bond of connexion with the covenant, which might exist without
the natural, as well as the natural without the spiritual. The necessity of a spiritual relation to God
could not be dispensed with; but where this existed,
the accident of birth was not of essential moment.
Wherever any one possessed Abraham's faith, he
could not fail to be received by an unchangeable and
impartial God to the place and portion of a son of
Abraham. It was just as competent for the people
of Edom, or Moab, or Nineveh, to enter thus into the
bond of Abraham's covenant, as for any of his natural posterity; and, in dealing graciously with the one,
the Lord at the same time stretched out his hand to
the other. In manifest proof of this, not only were
Abraham's servants at the first circumcised, and

thereby entitled to take up their standing with himself as heirs of blessing, but express provision was made in the law for strangers from the surrounding countries being circumcised and forming part of the Lord's heritage.—(Exod. xii. 44; Deut. xxiii. 1-8.) The temple also was, with the same view, named " the house of prayer for all nations" (1 Kings viii. 41-43; Isa. lvi. 7); and examples of pious converts, such as the father-in-law of Moses, Ruth, Ittai the Gittite, and thousands besides in the more flourishing periods of Israel's history, were from time to time added to the number of Abraham's seed. So that this seed, or the true Church of God in Old Testament times, though always Israelitish in name, was by no means exclusively Israelitish in origin, and that it did not consist more than was actually the case, of those converted naturalized Israelites—that all the surrounding nations, indeed, did not press into the kingdom of God, arose from no unwillingness on the part of God to receive them, but merely from their own unwillingness to come; for it was from the first *his* design, that they should see in Israel the way to blessing, and, like the young Moabite widow, should go " to put their trust under the wings of the Lord God of Israel."

The principle on which the whole of this proceeded is as fresh and operative still, let it be remembered, as it ever was in days of old; it partakes of the unchangeableness of Jehovah. What he has at any time done for one, he is ready to repeat to others similarly situated. In his communications to the father of the faithful, we may discern an assurance of his goodness to ourselves, and a divine warrant to look for like manifestations of grace in our own experience. On the other hand, the evils threatened or inflicted upon those who lived in unbelief, or fell back from their covenant engagements, should sound as warnings in our ear not to be high-minded but to fear, and to remember that, if we stand in grace, still by grace only can we stand. And hence it is that the apostle Paul could so readily bring forward, in proof of the doctrine that God was calling a church, "not of the Jews only, but also of the Gentiles," a passage from Hosea which was originally addressed to the natural Israel. " As he saith also in Hosea, I will call them my people, which were not my people; and her beloved, which was not beloved. And it shall come to pass, that in the place where it was said unto them, Ye are not my people; there shall they be called the children of the living God."—(Rom. ix. 24–26.) This, we are to bear in mind, the apostle cites as a direct and conclusive proof that Gentile or uncircumcised believers were as certainly called of God as converted Jews. And the only conceivable ground on which he could do so, is simply this, that God's communications of mercy and judgment to ancient Israel were a revelation to mankind at large; and that as Israel, in apostatizing, fell substantially into the condition of the heathen, so the promise of his reception again, on conversion, into the family of

God, was equally a promise of the reception of all believing Gentiles into the same family. For God would otherwise have acted from caprice, and his dealings could not have been, what, however, they must always be, the manifestations of his own holy and unchangeable nature.

CHAPTER III

IF it seemed strange, at first sight, that Jonah should
have received a commission from the Lord to go to
Nineveh, his conduct on receiving the commission
appears yet more strange: "But Jonah," it is said
with perfect simplicity, and without any attempt
either to explain or to justify his behaviour, "Jonah
rose up to flee unto Tarshish from the presence of the
Lord, and went down to Joppa; and he found a ship
going to Tarshish: so he paid the fare thereof, and
went down into it, to go with them unto Tarshish
from the presence of the Lord." This, we believe, is
the only case on record of a true prophet being
charged with the deliverance of a distinct and solemn
message from the Lord, and yet proving so unfaithful
to the charge as to take upon himself the fearful risk
of keeping the message concealed in his own bosom.
We have no reason to doubt, however, that there
were instances of unfaithfulness in the prophetical, as

well as the priestly order in Israel, to the extent, at least, of not maintaining the protest against error, and denouncing the judgments of heaven against sin, with the frequency and boldness which became the office. In this respect the prophets, more especially after the institution of the schools of the prophets, to which they usually belonged, and by which they were formed into a distinct order, had much the same part to fulfil that now devolves on ministers of the gospel. They were special, authorized teachers of the church, charged with the duty of expounding the law of God, and applying it to the ever-varying condition and circumstances of the people. This was the case to a considerable extent, at least in later times, even in the kingdom of Judah; but in the kingdom of Israel, where the priesthood was corrupt to the core, and their ministrations were utterly rejected by God, the prophetical order assumed a still more regular and organized character, and the prophets had to do much that properly belonged to the priesthood. Thus we find Elijah on Mount Carmel even officiating as a priest at the altar; and from an incidental notice in the history of the Shunamite woman respecting Elisha, it would appear that the prophets were in the habit of presiding at religious meetings on Sabbath-days and new moons.—(2 Kings iv. 23). It would also appear from a fact stated at the close of the same chapter— the fact of a man from Baal-shalisha bringing to Elisha bread of the first-fruits—that the dues of the priesthood (of which these first-fruits formed a part,

Deut. xviii. 4, 5) were paid to the prophets by the pious remnant among whom they then ministered in Israel.

This being the case, however, in the kingdom of Israel—the prophets there having in the first instance to act the part of public guardians, expounders, and teachers of the law of God—we can easily understand how, in this department at least of their official duties, they may occasionally have given way to a spirit of slumber, and have become chargeable with unfaithfulness. Their calling, in this view of it, very nearly coincided with that of a minister of the gospel, whose office, even when accompanied with suitable spiritual gifts, affords no security against partial shortcomings and failures in duty. We even find an occasion recorded in New Testament scripture, on which an apostle, though occupying in respect of office a much higher position than either a Christian minister or an ancient prophet, was sharply reproved for unfaithfulness in duty by another apostle.—(Gal. ii.) And those who in the church at Corinth were supernaturally endowed with prophetical gifts, are plainly charged by St Paul with a certain measure of misdirection and abuse in the application that was made of them.—(1 Cor. xiv.)

It would therefore be against all analogy to suppose, that the prophets in Old Testament times uniformly exercised the divine gift committed to them with unfailing promptitude and fidelity. It was doubtless possible for them, not less than for private believers, to resist the promptings, or even altogether to quench the agency, of the Spirit that wrought in them. One case, in particular, is recorded of most flagrant misconduct in a prophet, the old man at Bethel, who, under the false pretence of having received a special communication from heaven, induced another prophet —the one sent from Judah to denounce the judgment of heaven upon the altar erected by Jeroboam and the priests that served at it—to return and eat with him against an express injunction to the contrary.— (1 Kings xiii.) Such extraordinary behaviour on the part of that old prophet at Bethel, can scarcely be accounted for otherwise than on the supposition of a sort of convulsive effect having been produced upon his mind by the holy daring of the prophet from Judah, which contrasted so strongly with his own past unfaithfulness. For residing, as he did, at Bethel, the very scene of the new-enacted idolatry, it properly belonged to him to protest against the unrighteous innovation; for *that* he needed no direct revelation from heaven, as so many existing revelations bore upon the subject: he needed only a spirit of fearless and uncompromising allegiance to Jehovah; but not possessing this himself, and learning of a sudden, how nobly and with what approving signs from heaven it had been displayed by the prophet of Judah, he was seized with such a passionate desire of being honoured with the fellowship of that more faithful and distinguished brother, that he was resolved at all hazards to compass his return to Bethel.

At the same time, cases of delinquency, such as

those referred to, must certainly be regarded as belonging to an inferior kind of prophetical unfaithfulness
as compared with the direct disobedience of Jonah.
In the former, there was no special commission
violated ; the prophet merely failed to exercise the
authority with which he was invested to lift up the
testimony against sin, which God's word had already
delivered and put into his hands.   The case certainly
was different, and the transgression considerably more
aggravated, when there was an immediate revelation
from heaven, pointing out a particular field for the
exercise of the prophetic agency, and a definite message given to be delivered there, and yet no attempt
made to execute the solemn charge.   Such, however,
was Jonah's case.   Disobedient to the heavenly
vision, " he rose up to flee from the presence of the
Lord," and went down to Joppa to take ship in a
vessel bound for Tarshish (a city either on the coast
of Spain, or the opposite coast of Africa, hence lying
in a nearly contrary direction to Nineveh), " to go with
them to Tarshish from the presence of the Lord."

We are doubtless not to imagine Jonah so utterly
foolish and ignorant in this effort to escape from an
incumbent duty, as to suppose, that by flying to
Tarshish he thought he might entirely evade the
notice or oversight of God.   We have only to suppose, that he was extremely reluctant to undertake
the work imposed on him, and that he conceived it
might possibly be allowed to fall into abeyance, if he
could effect his removal to a distance from the region

where the prophetic agency of God's Spirit displayed itself. "He imagined," to use the words of the Jewish commentator, Kimchi, "that if he went out of the land of Israel, the Spirit of prophecy would not rest upon him." And making due allowance for the change that has taken place in outward circumstances, and in the mode of the Spirit's working, the behaviour of Jonah does not seem to have differed materially from the conduct of those in Christian times who are divinely prompted from within, or in the course of providence are distinctly called to the performance of some important work of reformation, but morbidly shrink from the scene of labour, on account of the real or fancied difficulties which appear to surround it, and determinately cling to a place of comparative seclusion or retirement. *

What the considerations actually were which pressed so heavily upon the mind of Jonah, and led

* In such cases, there usually (though we can scarcely say *always*) is some degree of uncertainty whether there actually be a call of God, or at least there is some room left for the individual himself to doubt whether there be such a call, as renders it impossible for him to decline without directly contravening the will of Heaven. It is perfectly possible, however, that Jonah himself may have found some such loophole in the manner or time of the communication made to him respecting Nineveh. But viewed simply in respect to the state of mind which gave rise to the desire or purpose of evasion, it does not appear that Jonah's case very essentially differed from that of Moses, when, after being driven from all his objections, he still sought to be relieved from the task of conducting Israel out of Egypt, as a work from which *he* at least must be excused. That he did not actually flee, like Jonah, from the appointed scene of labour

him to disobey so plain a command of God, we are
left in great measure to conjecture.   One reason he
has himself alleged near the conclusion of the book,
where it is introduced in connexion with the disappointment he experienced at the preservation of
Nineveh :—" I pray thee, O Lord, was not this my
saying, when I was yet in my country ?   Therefore I
fled before unto Tarshish ; for I knew that thou art
a gracious God, and merciful, slow to anger, and of
great kindness, and repentest thee of the evil."   It is
not altogether clear how Jonah intended this saying
to be understood as a motive for his flight toward
Tarshish ; but the construction put upon it by Jerome,
though concurred in by several of the fathers, certainly
goes in the wrong direction : " The prophet knew,
through the inward suggestion of the Holy Spirit,
that the repentance of the Gentiles would be the
ruin of the Jews.   Therefore, as a lover of his

arose more from the overawing manifestation of divine displeasure, than from any principle of duty yet working in his mind.
In modern times also, we might refer to the illustrious Calvin,
who, when urged to settle at Geneva as one peculiarly qualified
to carry forward and complete the work of reformation there,
was only arrested and brought off from his purpose of retirement
and study by the terrible address of Farel, which seized him, he
says, like the dreadful hand of God : " If you thus make your
own studies a pretext for not assisting us in this work of God, I
denounce to you in the name of Almighty God, that his curse
shall cleave to you, as you are seeking self rather than Christ."
In such momentous undertakings, the greatest spirits are at first
apt to misgive; indeed often none so apt as they; for they see
more clearly than others the mighty interests involved, and the
giant effort needed to effect the desired result.

country, he was not so much displeased at the thought of Nineveh's salvation, as he was averse to the destruction of his own people;" as if the conversion of the Gentiles of necessity inferred the rejection of Israel, and were not rather to be regarded by a heaven-taught man as an important and distinguishing element in their coming glory.* Far different thoughts were likely to crowd upon the mind of Jonah, when the formidable task was imposed upon him of going to do the work of a reformer in the vast metropolis of Assyria, and such as were more fitted to call forth the pity and forbearance of Heaven in respect to the wayward and erring course to which they impelled him. " Alas!" we can suppose him to have said within himself, " what can I hope to accomplish as the bearer of God's message against the crying sins and abominations of Nineveh? I, a soli-

---

* Gen. xii. 3, xxii. 18, xlix. 10; Deut. xxxii. 43; Ps. xlv., lxvii., lxviii., &c. The main stream of prophecy up till the time of Jonah in relation to the Gentiles, represented their dependence upon Israel for blessing, and pointed to the period of their actually coming to participate with Israel in their good. It is somewhat strange, and was no doubt partly owing to the loose typological views current in his age, that Lightfoot should have overlooked this prevailing current of prophecy up to the time of Jonah, and should have so readily acquiesced in the superficial opinion of Jerome. In his *Chronica Temporum*, he accounts, first, for the position of the book of Jonah after those of Hosea, Joel, Amos, and Obadiah, on the ground that these had respect to the destruction and desolation of Israel and Judah, together with Esau, while Jonah's has respect to the calling of the Gentiles; and, secondly, for Jonah's unwillingness to go to Nineveh, on the score of love to his own people, precisely as Jerome.

tary individual, a poor and unknown stranger, in the midst of a proud, overgrown city, revelling in wealth and wantonness! What success have I had at home even among the people of my own tongue and nation? Here, with every advantage on my side, I have borne the testimony of God in vain, and have seen the hand of the Lord stretched out to save from impending ruin, with no other effect among the people at large than of giving new wings to profligacy and corruption. My soul is already sick with looking at the things which have been proceeding around me; my hands hang down nerveless and enfeebled, because of the fruitlessness of their past exertions; and yet I am the man to be sent to deal with that mighty mass of pride and unrestrained wickedness! Is there the least likelihood of their listening to my voice? Will they not rather taunt me, if I should for a moment gain their ear, with the continued impenitence of my own people, and my unavailing efforts to reclaim them? And, whatever success might attend my labours when transferred to that distant field, will not He who has so long spared Israel under so many provocations, much more spare them? Why may not matters, then, be allowed to take their course? Or, if the call to repentance must be proclaimed, let it be at least committed to one better prepared for the toils and difficulties of the undertaking."

Such, we can readily suppose, might be the train of reflection that would press upon the mind of Jonah in the peculiarly trying circumstances in which he was now placed. It is true, neither the difficulties before nor the discouragements behind, which thus hung like a heavy and chilling cloud upon his soul, were sufficient to justify his refusal to deliver the Lord's message in Nineveh; faith should have made him deaf to every remonstrant feeling, and should have carried him in triumph over the fears and misgivings which so naturally assailed him. But the situation in which he was placed was one of singular, almost unprecedented difficulty—commissioned, as he was, to a work which required the most dauntless courage and buoyant energy of spirit, while he was inwardly crushed with vexation at the incurable blindness and obstinacy of his own people. A sinking of the soul in such circumstances, and even a shrinking back for the moment from the appointed task, however deserving of rebuke in the eye of God, is never to be placed on a level with backslidings and transgressions of an ordinary kind. And to apply here, as is so frequently done, to the son of Amittai the narrow measuring-line of common rules and " modern instances," and then to deal out against him such railing accusation as might suit only the most perverse and inexcusable offenders, is simply to betray one's ignorance of the affecting peculiarities of his case, or one's inability to sympathize with the troubles of a soul reeling and staggering under its weighty load of sore discouragements and overwhelming obligations.

With such a view of Jonah's situation, we see no

occasion to wonder, with certain moralizers on his
history, that, notwithstanding his present failing, he
should still be reckoned among the true prophets and
eminent servants of God; far less are we disposed to
concur with certain others, who seem almost to grudge
him a place at all in the number of the saints.   But,
on the other hand, we are as far from being disposed
to deny that his conduct merited the rod of chastisement; nor was he long in finding it applied with
righteous severity, though the judgment, as might
have been expected in the circumstances, was graciously tempered with mercy.   Indeed, it was an act
of mercy to employ any means to check him in his
course; for the worst thing that can be done to a
transgressor, is to let him alone in his transgression.
The adversary of souls could wish for nothing more
favourable to his designs; and, though he is himself
incapable of doing or desiring any thing in itself good,
we can yet suppose him looking on with malignant
satisfaction, when the child of disobedience is seen
swimming in prosperity, as if borne on the propitious
gales of heaven, while still drifting with fatal certainty on the rocks of perdition.

Such delusive prosperity, however, can never be
more than temporary.   The truth cannot be long in
making itself known, that " the righteous Lord
loveth righteousness," and that " the way of transgressors is hard"——the more hard if, by the greatness
of their privileges, or the dignity of their calling,
they have come to occupy a relation of peculiar near-

ness to God. For the closer their connexion with him, the more quick and immediate must always be the flashes of divine resentment upon them, when they presume to resist the claims of the divine authority. Least of all was it possible for such a person as Jonah to be allowed to prosper in his waywardness; a prophet raised up to be a guide to others, and yet himself taking the path of transgression! He of all men must be checked in his career. And so "the Lord sent out a great wind into the sea, and there was a mighty tempest in the sea, so that the ship was like to be broken."

That one, who knew so well the all-pervading presence and controlling providence of God, should have imagined he could be safe in committing himself to the waves of ocean, when flying as a rebel from the appointment of Him who made that "swelling deep," as well as "the dry land," is an astonishing proof of the blinding influence of sin. In the very simplest elements of his faith, there was enough to condemn Jonah of flagrant misconduct. But we may not, on that account, wantonly aggravate the greatness of his guilt. We have no ground to affirm, and it is against all probability to suppose, that his conscience was already lulled into a profound sleep, and that it plied him with no upbraidings of remorse. We are not warranted to regard the deep slumber in which he lay when the storm rose upon the ship, as the symptom of a benumbed and stupified heart, but should rather ascribe it, in so far as any *moral* cause

may have contributed to its production, to the depressed and dislocated state of his mind, arising from the
painful struggle with convictions of duty through
which he had passed.   The whole we can with confidence say of this part of his history is, that the
divine retribution was swifter than his own appre-
hensions of danger; and that he was actually surrounded with the deep waters before he was conscious
of their approach.   But he was soon to be aroused as
with a voice of thunder; for when all efforts failed to
contend against the storm, or to secure the vessel
from destruction—when the angry elements, waxing
continually more violent and threatening, forced on
the minds of all, doubtless through the directing
agency of the Spirit, a conviction of some one being
in the vessel whom the vengeance of heaven was
pursuing with evil*—and when the trial by lot was
resorted to for the purpose of ascertaining who the
guilty individual might be, and the lot fell upon
Jonah—then he felt the arrest of God's hand upon
him.   "Thou art the man," resounded in his inmost
soul; and in the tempest, that raged with so much
fury, he at once recognized and owned the instrument
of vengeance to punish his iniquity.

   We cannot but admire the frankness of Jonah's

---

   * How near such a thought was to the ancient heathen appears
from the words of Horace, Car. iii. 2, v. 26 :—

      — Vetabo, qui Cereris sacrum
   Vulgârit arcanæ, sub îsdem
      Sit trabibus, fragilemque mecum
   Solvat phaselon.   Sæpe Diespiter, &c.

confession of guilt, and his willing surrender to the claims of justice, when the temptations were so great to an opposite course—an evidence surely of something very different from a sophisticated mind or a seared conscience. When thus directly called in providence to consider his ways, we hear of no shuffling excuses or dishonest evasions, but only the unreserved utterance of a heart already conscious of its guilt, and itself the foremost to pronounce judgment on the offence. But the situation of Jonah, when so detected by the singular providence of God, and constrained to witness to his own condemnation, was of the most sad and humiliating description. "A righteous man," says Solomon, "falling down before the wicked, is as a troubled fountain and a corrupt spring." Here was a righteous man fallen in the worst sense—fallen from his righteousness : more than that, a prophet specially raised up and supernaturally endowed for advancing among men the interests of God's kingdom—one who, by his wholesome instructions and exemplary character, should have been as a crystal spring, sending forth all around streams of living water, yet found an occasion of trouble and distress, a terror to himself and a bane to others ! When the chief prophet of God to Israel, and his chosen representative to the world, lay thus prostrate as a detected and doomed sinner before a company of heathen mariners, how entirely did the foundations of the earth seem to be out of course ! O unhappy Israel ! have thy backslidings mounted so high as to reach even the ambassadors of heaven within thy borders? How near must thou be to destruction, when thy very lights are thus dimming their brightness, thy standard-bearers fainting and falling down in confusion before the heathen, who should have stood with awe in their presence, and, from fellowship with them, should have derived only life and blessing!

Such reflections naturally force themselves on our minds in connexion with so grievous a fall in the high places of Israel. The work of God required a man of high-strung energy and noble elevation of soul, and Jonah, at this stage of his career, proved inadequate to the occasion; he sinks like a fragile vessel beneath the burden which the Spirit of God had deemed it needful to impose on him. But he is not alone in the condemnation; he bears upon his soul the iniquities also of those with whom he is connected—Israel behind, and now Nineveh before; his miserable failure is but the reflection of their widespread degeneracy and manifold provocations, as was formerly the case with Moses at the waters of Meribah;* for it was his vexing and unfruitful connexion with a people bent on backsliding, that had

---

* Deut. iv. 21. The Lord is there said to have been "angry with Moses for their sakes," as it is in our version; but as it should rather be, "on account of their words," viz., the murmuring and rebellious words they spoke at Meribah. What Hengstenberg has correctly noted on the connexion of Moses and Aaron with the guilt of the people, may substantially be applied also to Jonah: "The guilt of the leaders is plainly to be recog-

brought such faintness upon his spirit and such back-sliding into his course; so that in his declension was proclaimed the solemn lesson, " the whole head is sick, the whole heart is faint."

This thought, however, was rather for Israel at large than for Jonah himself, since it could not properly excuse or justify, however it might in part account for, his present humiliating and perilous condition. Therefore it never comes at all into notice here. When the mariners asked Jonah why he had done so, he was silent as to any justification of himself; their question is recorded, but not his answer, for he had none to give. And when they again asked him, " What shall we do unto thee, that the sea may be calm to us ?" his reply was at hand : " Take me up, and cast me forth into the sea; so shall the sea be calm to you : for I know that for my sake this great tempest is upon you." His companions in trouble had now got full permission to do their worst upon him ; but, partly won by the simplicity and frankness of Jonah's behaviour, and partly overawed by the manifestation of divine justice which was proceeding before their eyes, they still strove to avert the calamity which seemed to be inevitable. Anxious, if possible, to save this stranger's life, and afraid lest

nized as the result of that of the people. Without the unbelief of the latter, there had not been the exhibition of weakness on the part of the former. Faint and wearied by the long course of provocations, they were at last, in a moment of weakness, carried away by the stream of the popular spirit of defection."— (*Authentie*, ii. p. 426.)

the vengeance which seemed to pursue him for having sinned against God in one respect should fall upon them by sinning in another, "they rowed hard to bring the ship to land." Their efforts, however, were in vain; and when, at last, no alternative appeared to be left but that of executing the awful doom, they proceeded to it with a trembling heart, and a solemn appeal to Heaven for the integrity of their purpose: "We beseech thee, O Lord, we beseech thee, let us not perish for this man's life, and lay not upon us innocent blood: for thou, O Lord, hast done as it pleased thee. So they took up Jonah, and cast him forth into the sea: and the sea ceased from her raging."

Behold, then, the severity of God! how sternly impartial in its executions of judgment! It was not enough that Jonah had become alive to his transgression, and condemned himself on account of it; nay, while the men around him melt at the thought of his fate, and would fain have it averted, there is no relenting on the part of Heaven, but a rigorous enforcement of the demands of justice. Why such painful severity here? Because the ends of the divine government required it—required it, in the first instance, for Jonah himself: he had sinned presumptuously against God, and he must bear the penalty; it was a righteous thing for God in such a case to inflict, and for him to yield to the appointed doom. But still more was this example of severity needed for the good of others. The honour and cause of

God were at the time peculiarly bound up with the faithfulness of Jonah ; and, having failed in the way of duty to promote the glory of God, he must in another way become instrumental in advancing it—he must be *made*, by the things he suffered, a witness for God's righteousness, since he had ceased to *do* the part of a witness by the active performance of the duty required of him. We thus learn from his experience, that near relationship to God purchases no immunity to sin ; it only ensures, when sin is indulged, a speedier execution of judgment : so that, if the shepherd of the Lord's flock should prove unmindful of his charge, or the Church itself should as a whole, or in any of its members, become backsliding and corrupt, there especially must God show himself in severity ; he is pre-eminently dishonoured there, and the work of judgment must proceed, that others may see and fear.

But in what presently befell Jonah we are also called to behold the goodness of God ; for no sooner is he cast out, as a victim of divine justice, into the raging deep, than a great fish was ready to swallow him up—not for instant destruction, but for safe preservation. The peaceful elements of nature had been lashed into fury when the means of chastisement were required ; and now, when a purpose of mercy was to be accomplished, the devourer was at once transformed into a house of safety—a proof, both ways, of the infinite resources of God, and how easy it is for him to provide himself any where with the instruments

required for the execution of his designs. What precisely the great fish might be,* or why exactly this
mode of preservation might be resorted to, it is of
little moment to inquire.   In the act of preservation
there certainly was a miraculous display of the power
of God; and the particular mode of doing it seems
to have been adopted with the view of rendering
Jonah's condition, while under punishment, as much
as possible an emblem of death. With such guilt
upon him, he *should* have died; and, although he was
miraculously spared, yet the means employed for his
preservation formed a kind of temporary death—as he
seems, from the moment of his ejection into the sea,
to have lost all further consciousness of life, to have
felt simply as a drowning man, plunged into the deep
waters, and no longer numbered among the living.
The whole was ordered with a special view to his
being constituted such a *sign*, both to the generation
then living and to future times, as the purposes of

* The view commonly adopted from the earliest times has
understood by the great fish *a whale*—although it is well known
that the Hebrew word here, and even the corresponding Greek
word in Matt. xii. 40, is applicable to *any* great fish. The nar-
rowness of the neck of the whale has led many commentators to
think of some other fish—Bochart the dog-fish, and others some
species of shark; and yet in whales there is another cavity besides the stomach—a sort of huge air-vessel, which might have
been made to serve the purpose.—(See Jebb's *Sacred Literature*,
p. 178.)   But recent writers have wisely given up speculations of
this kind; a miracle any way was needed; and that various large
fishes might be found in the Mediterranean suitable for the
purpose, is no longer a matter of doubt.

Divine wisdom required.   And to this our thoughts must now be turned—but not till we have first descended with Jonah into this valley of the shadow of death, to learn from him what lessons of wisdom his experience there has furnished for the Church and people of God.

CHAPTER IV

JONAH IN HIS DISTRESS AN EXAMPLE OF SANCTIFIED AFFLICTION.

It is always interesting, and may be profitable as well as interesting, to mark the workings of a soul when struggling with the strong billows of affliction, especially if that affliction has come in the immediate train of backsliding, and appears as the net in which God has caught a wanderer from the fold, or the rod by which would bring him back to wisdom and obedience. The effect would be quite uniform: the means would always reach their intended aim, if in the persons so dealt with there were always the elements of a sincere and living piety. This, however, is far from being the case. And hence there is a class of professing Christians, in whom even the heaviest afflictions are found to work no spiritual good—the flesh bruised, but still the spirit not sanctified; earthly delights cut off with a stroke, but yet no springs of heavenly consolation opened up; a valley of Baca, but without its wells of living water; a wilderness with no manna from above, or Canaan in prospect;

a sorrow that either works death or leads with delusive hope to new refuges of lies. A sad case truly,
when the medicine of God's righteous discipline makes
itself known only in its bitterness, or tends but to
deepen the wound it was intended to cure.

But, on the other hand, when the life of grace has
really obtained a footing in the soul, another and hap-
pier result is sure to flow from the visitation of severe
distress. Earnest thought, a spirit of serious reflection, is awakened. The voice of conscience makes
itself heard in the chambers of the inner man; and
if any delusive charm has been laying the spell of its
enchantment upon the heart, the spell is broken, truth
and reason regain their rightful ascendant—the soul
lives again to God. Such, pre-eminently, was the result of " the horror of great darkness" which fell upon
Jonah, and his descent under God's judgment into the
bowels of the earth, as the record of his experience
amply testifies: "And Jonah prayed unto the Lord
his God out of the fish's belly. And said, I cried by
reason of mine affliction unto the Lord, and he heard
me; out of the belly of hell* cried I, and thou heardest
my voice. For thou hadst cast (or, hast cast) me into
the deep, in the midst of the seas; and the floods
compassed me about: all thy billows and thy waves
passed over me. Then I said, I am cast out of thy

---

* Literally, out of the womb of *Sheol:* or, more generally, the
interior of the place of the departed; implying, along with the
expressions in v. 6, that he felt as if actually in the state of the
dead.

sight; yet I will look again toward thy holy temple. The waters compassed me about,* even to the soul: the depth closed me round about, the weeds were wrapped about my head. I went down to the bottoms of the mountains; the earth with her bars was about me for ever; yet hast thou brought up my life from corruption, O Lord my God.† When my soul fainted within me (or rather, because of the over-whelming of my soul upon me) I remembered the Lord : and my prayer came in unto thee, into thy holy temple. They that observe (regard) lying vanities forsake their own mercy.‡ But I will sacrifice to thee

* The verbs here should properly be rendered in the present tense: "The waters compass me about," &c. For though the prayer might not be composed till he came out of the fish, yet it expresses what he thought and felt while in it.

† This verse admits of various emendations, and would be more correctly rendered thus: "I have gone down to the roots (or clefts) of the mountains; the earth ! her bars are about me for ever. And thou shalt bring up my soul from the pit, O Jehovah my God." In the first clause, the prophet expresses the hope-lessness of his condition, as having gone to a depth from which he had no power to rise up again. In the second, he glances to the earth, the habitation of the living, and sees only its bars impe-netrably shut against him; but in the third, he turns to God, and expresses his confidence, that even from that pit of death the divine power and mercy would recover him. The שחת from which he expects to be brought up, is falsely rendered *corruption*, and also still by Henderson *destruction;* its common, or rather its *only* meaning is the *pit*, (see Hengstenberg on Ps. xvi. 10), used here, as elsewhere, in the sense of the grave. Jonah regards himself as actually among the dead.

‡ The last clause should be, "forsake their Loving-kindness," this being understood as an epithet of God. The expression is

with the voice of thanksgiving; I will pay what I have vowed. Salvation is of the Lord."

Now, viewing the thoughts and feelings expressed in this prayer as a proof that Jonah's affliction was truly sanctified to him—the light in which they ought chiefly to be regarded—there are a few leading points that more especially deserve our consideration.

1. *First*, we remark the altered feeling toward God of which he was now conscious, as compared with that state of mind which tempted him to go astray. In the former respect it is said of him, " he rose up to flee from the presence of the Lord;" he felt too near, as it were, to Jehovah, and would fain withdraw to a greater distance, that so he might escape from a burden which pressed like an iron yoke upon his neck. But now it is one of the bitterest parts of his complaint that he was so far from God: " I said, I am cast out from thy sight,"—driven away, as it more literally is, from before thine eyes. He has got in this respect his desire; God has retired to a distance from him; but ah! instead of finding it to be well with him on that account, the thought of God's averted countenance becomes insupportably painful. How sweet now would it be to him to dwell amid the beams of that countenance! for he sees God as he never did before, in an aspect of tenderness and

taken from Ps. cxliv. 2, where David styles God " my goodness," or loving-kindness, חסדי : God, who is to me all beneficence— " Love;" so also, in Ps. lix. 17, " The God of my mercy," or, more correctly, " my kindness-God."

love; the very idea of God is identified with loving-kindness, and the attempt to seek comfort by going into estrangement from him appears only as a species of infatuation or madness.

It must, indeed, be a sanctified trouble which disposes the soul to feel thus toward God—to eye him as a loving Father at the very time he is applying the rod of chastisement, and to charge all the blame of the severity of the dealing upon its own wayward-ness and folly. This is not the way of unrenewed nature. Where it alone works, there may possibly be no rising against the authority or fretting at the appointment of God—there may be the exercise of a spirit of subduing fear and quiet resignation; but actually to cherish kind thoughts of God, and be conscious of a drawing affection toward him—to see him lovely and good, and feel that in his favour is life, while still his providence is dark and frowning—this can be found only with the child of grace, who has the Spirit of God, quickening the heart to love, and sanctifying the rod of affliction. He who is in this condition, but he alone, has come to regard God as the only good, and a state of separation and dis-tance from him as the worst of evils.

2. It was but the natural consequence of this state of mind in Jonah, though it may be noted as another mark of his sanctified affliction, that he poured out his heart in prayer: the Spirit of sonship was again revived in him, and it led him to cry, Abba, Father. And it is worthy of remark, that we are not told

this of him before he reached the extremity of his distress. We have seen him in great danger, in profound slumber, under deep convictions of sin, adjudging himself, in agony of spirit, to the doom of an outcast; but only now, when shut up in the deep waters, do we hear of his having sought to God in prayer. For he had knowingly taken the part of a backslider from God; and in nothing does backsliding more readily discover itself than in the loss of familiarity with Heaven; consciousness of sin excludes nearness and freedom of communion; "prayer is restrained before God," the very form not unfrequently abandoned; and, even where that in some degree is retained, still the life is utterly gone—no thirsting of the soul after God and the things of his salvation. But now when the work of severity has effected its end, and a truly chastened heart has been wrought in Jonah, he begins to cry in earnest to the Lord; he becomes, in the strictest sense, a man of prayer.

What is this but the man returning to his proper place again? He has wandered as a lost child, but says, "I will arise and go to my Father." What prompts the return, and gives it this salutary direction? What, but the bruising influence of the rod— the felt want and desolation of soul, which can find relief nowhere else than in God? It is not prosperity, which we naturally so much covet and run after, that does this; nay, thousands have been carried by that into forgetfulness of God, and tempted to leave off habits of communion with him which they once possessed, endangered most of all by the fulness of their condition and the smoothness of their course. Not prosperity, therefore, but affliction; yet this only when sanctified by grace to discover the vanity of the world, to wean the heart from its fleshly confidences, and awaken it to the necessity of a life " that has some relish of salvation in it." "This poor man cried"—cried just because, under the discipline of God, he had come to know himself to be poor— " and the Lord heard him." " In their affliction they will seek me early;" they fled from me before, but now they will be in haste to find me and call upon my name. So that we may certainly conclude of affliction generally, if it drives the heart from its idols, if it breaks the spirit of self-sufficiency, if it brings a man to his knees, it is an affliction sanctified for his spiritual good.

3. But, more particularly, we have to mark the workings of faith here, sanctified affliction being always characterized by the degree in which faith is called into exercise. The prayer itself is entitled to notice on this ground; for what was it in the case of Jonah, or what is sincere prayer in any case but the fruit of faith? Yet it is not so much the simple act of prayer, as rather the particular views and feelings which are expressed in prayer, or otherwise manifested, that mainly indicate the faith which should be found in the school of affliction.

(1.) In this respect we have to note, *first*, the exercise of faith in regard to the appointment of the visitation. Jonah was at no loss to discover the quarter from which his overwhelming troubles came upon him; it was not accident or some unknown power, but the hand of God which had ordained them: "*Thou* hast cast me into the deep;" "*thy* waves and *thy* billows have passed over me." In like manner Job in the day of his calamity: "The Lord gave and the Lord hath taken away, blessed be the name of the Lord." So also David in the season of rebuke and blasphemy: "Let him curse, because the Lord hath said unto him, Curse David"—the man (Shimei) is but an instrument; that his malice takes this direction rather than any other is from the Lord; and, if I had not needed such a visitation of evil, it would not have been allowed to come upon me.

Such invariably is the feeling of the heart when it is enabled to exercise faith under the afflictions that press upon it; it looks above the immediate occasion or the particular circumstances, and feels that it has to do with Him who is through all and over all. As in the things we then experience there is a direct and special dealing with us on the part of God, so it is only when we are duly sensible of this, and acknowledge his hand in the appointment, that we are prepared to profit aright by the discipline, or to bear ourselves suitably under it. The thought of God's hand is especially fitted to quiet the turbulence of the heart when agitated with trouble, and check the rise of evil affections. No man who sees God in his dis-

tress, will be disposed to say, that he suffers more
than he deserves, or that the trials he experiences are
not wisely ordained for some good end. But if the
outward circumstances or immediate instruments
alone are considered, then fretting, discontent, or even
ebullitions of angry passion, will be ready to spring
up. I can say, perhaps, of a fellow-creature, He
should not have acted in such a manner toward me;
it was not the treatment I was entitled to expect from
him. But when I look higher, and see in the things
that befall me the operation of God's hand, I necessarily feel that silence is my becoming attitude; I
have now to do with infinite faithfulness and wisdom.
" It is the Lord, let him do what seemeth good to
him." " I was dumb because thou didst it."

(2.) As another exercise of Jonah's faith, and common with him to all afflicted saints, we must mark
his confidence and hope in God, not extinguished,
but rather roused into action, by the extremity of his
distress. Viewed simply in itself, his situation was
of the most desperate and forlorn description—an outcast from his fellow-men, from the habitable globe
itself, as being no longer fit to have a place among
the living—and that in consequence of the just judgment of Heaven, re-echoed and approved by the cry
of guilt in his own conscience, so that there seemed
to be almost every thing in his condition that might
bar the possibility of confidence and hope. Nor was
it by shutting his eyes on the evil that he found
relief to his mind; on the contrary, he takes the full

gauge of its dimensions, and pathetically laments that "he was cast into the deep," "cast out of God's sight;" he had turned his back on God, and now God, making his sin his punishment, turned his back on him; nay, made "*all* his waves and billows pass over him." For a time, indeed, he seems to have concluded, that all *was* completely over with him, that there was no room for hope, the daughter of faith, to enter; he had felt as if the earth's bars were about him for ever, and he was enclosed in the pit of all-devouring Sheol. But it was only for a time; "he remembered the Lord" when thus overwhelmed with perplexity; "he looked again toward God's holy temple," and cried in faith, and hoped for deliverance.

But faith must have some ground to stand upon, and some plea to urge. What had Jonah of this? Where had faith any thing on which to build its confidence and hope toward God? Why, simply in that he lived, and *could* look to the God to whom salvation belongs. He could say, "The Lord has chastened me sore, but not given me over to perdition; I live, and, while I live, I see my past folly, and turn again to the God of my life. There is mercy with Him, that he may be feared. His name is the Lord God, merciful and gracious. And why do I yet breathe? Why is sense and reflection still left to me in this place of dungeon-darkness? Is it not, that I might yet lay hold of God, and be found to his glory? I will therefore trust and hope in his mercy."

Faith is always, in proportion to its clearness and strength, fertile in resources; it is of quick discernment in the fear of the Lord, and will often find grounds of confidence and rays of hope, where to the natural mind all seems enveloped in gloom and despondency. The heart that is really inspired with faith, has that keen and lively relish for divine things which is ever found to be the best sharpener of the intellect, and "because it feels with enthusiasm, it penetrates with sagacity." Jonah had here the least possible ground to stand upon, but that little with faith was sufficient. The Syro-Phœnician woman with her great faith gathered strength to her confidence from the very things that seemed to the eye of sense to undermine it. " I am not sent," said Jesus, in answer to her suit, "but to the lost sheep of the house of Israel." True, thou art not *sent* elsewhere, but thou canst *go;* thou art the Son of David, the glorious king of Zion, and canst still, if thou pleasest, give what I ask—"Lord help me." "But it is not *meet* to take the children's bread, and cast it to the dogs." No, not meet, indeed, but neither do I ask it ; I am content to take but the dog's portion, for even they eat of the crumbs that fall from the table, and such is all I now supplicate.

There are times of trouble and distress, when the soul has thus to look down and search narrowly for its grounds of consolation and support—times when so many things are against it, that scarcely any special promise of Scripture appears altogether to meet its

case, and it has nothing but the *general* manifestations of God's character to fall back upon. Still,
however, at the very worst it has these, and the express warrant of the prophet to make use of them:
" Who is among you that feareth the Lord, that
obeyeth the voice of his servant, that walketh in
darkness, and hath no light? Let him trust in the
name (the manifested character) of the Lord, and
stay upon his God." Besides, such times of extreme
perplexity are comparatively of rare occurrence; for
the most part, no such difficulty need be felt; there
are grounds of consolation and words of promise
amply sufficient to meet the exigencies of the soul
when struggling amid the deep waters of affliction; and if grace truly mingles with the trial,
to sanctify the evil and call faith into exercise, it
will never fail to bring the soul in confidence and
hope to God.

(3.) There is a still further manifestation of faith in
the words of Jonah, and one which forms another
special mark of sanctified affliction; although it lies
less upon the surface than those already noticed, and
may even escape the observation of a hasty reader. I
refer to the use that is made of the earlier portions of
the word of God, and the recorded experiences of former times. It is but a brief prayer this of Jonah's,
the whole being comprised in eight short verses; and
yet it contains no fewer than seven quotations from
the Book of Psalms, which, more than any other book
of Scripture, is a record of the believer's experiences

and hopes in times of trouble.*   In a spirit of faith
Jonah identifies himself with the saints of former
times, so far as to appropriate to himself the language
that describes their trials and deliverances.   He looks
back to the footsteps of the flock as traced by the
fingers of inspired men, and sees there some gleams
of light to relieve the intense darkness that surrounded him.   The staggering thing to him at first was,
that his case was so remarkably peculiar; he was where
no one had ever been before; and if he could have be-

---

* I have said *seven* quotations, on the supposition that the
words in v. 2, "I cried by reason of mine affliction to the Lord,
and he heard me," are taken from Ps. cxx. 1, to which they very
nearly in our version, and in the original almost entirely, correspond.   But the date of that psalm is unknown, and it is quite
possible that it may not have been composed till a period posterior to the age of Jonah; so that the quotation may be from Jonah
by the psalmist, and not from the psalmist by Jonah.   There can
be no doubt about the others, which are all taken from psalms
belonging to the times of David, and pointing to the trials of his
own eventful life.   They are as follows: v. 3, "All thy billows
and thy waves passed over me," literally from Ps. xlii. 7; v. 4,
"And I said, I am cast out of thy sight," or, from before thine
eyes, with the change only of one letter in the original, from Ps.
xxxi. 22; v. 5, "The waters compassed me about to the soul,"
with the difference of only one word from Ps. lxix. 1; v. 7,
"When my soul fainted (was overwhelmed) within me," literally
from Ps. cxlii. 3; v. 8, "They that observe lying vanities," literally from Ps. xxxi. 6; v. 9, "Salvation is of the Lord," or is the
Lord's, from Ps. iii. 8.   Besides, there is a plain reference, as before noticed, to Ps. cxliv. 2, in the peculiar name that is applied
to God in v. 8, "loving-kindness;" and though the words are a
little different, yet the sentiment in the latter part of v. 7 is precisely the same with that in Ps. xviii. 6.

thought him of any saint that had ever been as low, and yet had been delivered, it would have gone far to re-assure and comfort his heart.   But lo! he does find this; he finds it in the word of the living God itself, which records experiences of others, not indeed altogether identical with his own, but so nearly alike, in all their essential features so much the same, that the words spoken of them were precisely those in which he could most fitly express the things that concerned himself.   In the volume of the book it was written even of him; for it was written of those who, like him, felt as if they had been cast out of God's sight— had been plunged in deep waters—rolled over by swelling waves and mighty billows, so that the waters came in to their very soul, and who yet in such great distresses cried to the Lord, and found him both able and willing to accomplish their deliverance.   How comforting for Jonah at such a time to find this! And how precious to him then that volume, in which there was contained for him the milk of such sweet consolation!

It is a great part of the design for which so many providential dealings and personal experiences have found a place in the inspired record, to furnish the means of such consolation in times of trial; and no small part of the wisdom and sagacity of faith consists in deriving at these times suitable and proper instruction from them.   Of the things written in this department, it may be emphatically said, " They were written for our learning, that we through patience and comfort of the Scriptures may have hope." As the Church of all ages is essentially one, so also is the manifested character of God; and whenever, or wherever, any child of God, and any portion of his Church, find themselves in a situation answerable to the testimonies recorded of past troubles or deliverances, they both may and ought to appropriate the language to themselves. For God is the same yesterday, to-day, and for ever; what he was, and what he has done in the past, he still is, and is ready to do in the future; and what he reveals of himself to one, he virtually declares to all to the very end of time.

In this appropriating use of the recorded experiences of former times, and the utterances of divine truth connected with them, not Jonah alone, but our blessed Lord himself, has left us an example of faith exercising itself thus under trial and temptation. As when, to refer only to one specimen, he replied to the solicitation of the tempter to turn a stone into bread, by saying, " It is written, Man shall not live by bread alone, but by every word that proceedeth out of the mouth of God." When and where was it so written? By Moses (in Deut. viii. 3), when rehearsing to the Israelites, at the close of their sojourn in the wilderness, the wonderful nature of God's dealings with them, and the support he miraculously provided through manna, when they were cut off from all ordinary supplies of food—" that he might make thee know (said the man of God), that man doth not live by bread only, but by every word that

proceedeth out of the mouth of God doth man live."
Might make *thee* know this, and with thee every
child of God to the latest time. Therefore did the
holy child Jesus take it in his state of wilderness
bereavement as a word of direction and promise to
him, not less than if it had been specially addressed
to himself ; and by his example he instructs us to do
the same, and to make a corresponding use of all the
memorials of God's past dealings with his people.
He bids us enter by faith into their history ; and,
when we are conscious of standing in a situation
similar to theirs, to make its lessons of wisdom or its
words of comfort our own—it is a revelation of God
to *us*.

But the instruction may also be applied with
greater latitude to the word of God at large. Not
some select portions merely, but that word as a whole
will always become precious, when affliction is truly
sanctified; faith will then be ever ready to repair
thither as to its storehouse to get counsel from the
Lord and replenish itself with arguments. " This is
my comfort in my affliction ; for thy word hath
quickened me." And again, " It is good for me
that I have been afflicted, that I might learn thy
statutes." As much as to say, I did not know till I
was in trouble and distress what was in thy word ; I
had but skimmed its surface, and knew not the depth
of meaning, the rich mine of instruction and blessing,
that is laid up in it. But I now know it ; my own
trials and necessities have opened out its infinite

suitableness to my condition, and taught me to appreciate its divine cordials, as well as to listen to its wholesome counsels. It is well to know the word of God at any time, even in the day of security and repose; for otherwise we shall not be prepared, in the season of peculiar need, to draw from it the strength and refreshment it is fitted to impart. But the full sense of its amazing richness and incomparable preciousness can be attained only in the school of tribulation. There then appears a reality, a felt adaptation to the wants and necessities of our case, in its tidings of mercy, its promises of love, even its darker representations, the sighs from the deep, the struggles of faith, the manifold alternations of fear and hope, through which it leads us—of which we were very imperfectly conscious before. The rod is blessed in the truest sense, when it thus brings us acquainted with the hidden treasures of wisdom and grace which lie enclosed in the word of God.

4. The last thing deserving of notice in the prayer of Jonah, as a mark of sanctified affliction, is the purpose of amendment it expresses. This rather runs through the whole of it, and appears in the altered tone of feeling it breathes toward God and his service, than comes distinctly out in any separate and formal announcements. We feel, it is impossible for us to doubt, while we read these meditations of his heart, that he is now cured of flying from God, and is resolutely bent on following the path of duty, wherever that may lead. Silently comparing his behaviour

in the past to the conduct of idolaters, those who
" regard lying vanities"—for whatever withdraws the
trust of the soul, and steals away the homage of its
affections from God, is in substance an idol, and as
such a delusive vanity, whose promises can end only
in disappointment and ruin—Jonah now declares his
conviction of the folly of such courses ; it is forsaking
for vain shadows the very source of love and beneficence ; and he therefore turns to God, whom he can
now regard also as the author of his salvation, with
the vow of thankful and devoted obedience. " I
will sacrifice to thee with the voice of thanksgiving ;
I will pay what I have vowed."

When trials and distresses are sent, as in the case
of Jonah, for correction and reproof in backsliding,
this is always of necessity the great end and issue to
which they point. They must, if not sent in vain,
work in us a thorough sense of the folly, as well as
guilt of sin, and of the wisdom and happiness, not
less than the duty, of obedience. While they do not
forbid us to count the cost of a dutiful surrender to
the will of God, they call us, with a voice of stern
rebuke, to count the incomparably greater cost of a
refusal, and seek to enforce upon our deceitful and
foolish hearts the salutary lesson, that if we would do
well to ourselves we must first do faithful and willing
service to God. Let the heart, therefore, of the believer ever say to itself, when cast by Christ into
the furnace of affliction : " My Lord sits here as a
refiner of silver ; he would have me entirely separated

from what mars the purity of my affections, and interferes with the integrity of my obedience. Let me fall in with his design, and, giving the dross of my corruption to be burnt up as in the fire of his judgment, devote myself anew as a living sacrifice to his fear; so that, if I must confess with the Psalmist, ' Before I was afflicted I went astray,' with him also I may be enabled to add, ' But *now* I keep thy word.' "

CHAPTER V

THE singular chapter of Jonah's history relating to
his descent into the fish's belly, and his restoration
alive, after a sojourn there of a part of three days, to
the habitable earth, was not intended to form a mere
excrescence or stray incident in his life, nor even a
special providence, without any other end in view than
the prophet's personal good. It was to be inwrought
as an essential element into his public character, and
was both intended and fitted to exert an important
bearing on his future calling and destiny. This we
learn beyond all doubt from the testimony of our
Lord himself, who on two separate occasions referred
to this remarkable period of Jonah's history, and
spake of the instruction with which it was fraught for
past and coming generations. The first occasion is
the one of which we have the fullest report in the
twelfth chapter of the gospel by Matthew. It formed
part of the transactions which arose out of the cure
of a poor demoniac—a cure that so impressed the

people with the supernatural power and glory of Jesus, that they instinctively said one to another, "Is not this the Son of David?" To nullify, if possible, this fatal conclusion, the Pharisees who were present resorted to the equally impious and unreasonable device of ascribing the power by which Jesus thus cast out devils, to Beelzebub the prince of the devils; which called forth from our Lord first an unanswerable exposure of the palpable absurdity of the supposition, then an awful warning in regard to the unpardonable sin of uttering blasphemy against the Holy Ghost, followed by a denunciation of the intense and hopeless malignity of those from whom such thoughts of wickedness proceeded. But some, it would appear, were not disposed to go altogether along with those, who imputed to Jesus such a revolting alliance with the powers of darkness, and yet were not satisfied with the supernatural proofs he had hitherto given of his Messiahship. These persons, therefore, who are called "certain of the Scribes and of the Pharisees," struck in at the close of our Lord's solemn discourse with the request, "Master, we would see a sign from thee;" which, in the corresponding passage of Luke's gospel (ch. xi. 16), is more explicitly called a sign from heaven: "And others, tempting him, sought of him a sign from heaven." "But he answered and said unto them," it is again written in Matthew, "An evil and adulterous generation seeketh after a sign; and there shall no sign be given to it but the sign of the prophet Jonas. For as Jonas was three days and three nights in the whale's belly, so shall the Son of man be three days and three nights in the heart of the earth. The men of Nineveh shall rise in judgment with this generation and shall condemn it, because they repented at the preaching of Jonas, and, behold, a greater than Jonas is here." Turning again, however, to the corresponding passage in the other evangelist, we find an important element added from the discourse of Christ on the occasion; for it is there stated, with respect no doubt to Jonah's sojourn for a time in the deep, that he was a sign to the Ninevites, as well as to the generation among whom our Lord lived: " As Jonas was a sign unto the Ninevites, so shall also the Son of man be to this generation." *

The other occasion on which our Lord pointed to the instruction contained in Jonah's temporary entombment in the fish's belly, occurred somewhat later in his history, and is noticed nowhere but at the commencement of the sixteenth chapter of St Matthew's gospel. We are there told, that " the Pharisees with the Sadducees came, and tempting, desired him that he would show them a sign from heaven." To which he first replied by rebuking them for their inability to discern the signs of the times, while they could

* The words in the original are somewhat more express than in our version, and denote, not merely that our Lord and Jonah were equally signs to the people among whom respectively they delivered the message of God, but that they were signs of the same kind (καθὼς ἐγένετο 'Ιωνᾶς), according as, or in the same manner " as Jonas was a sign to the Ninevites, so shall also the Son of man be to this generation."

so skilfully discern the face of the sky; and then referred them again to the prophet Jonah, but without
any note apparently of explanation : " A wicked and
adulterous generation seeketh after a sign: and there
shall no sign be given unto it but the sign of the prophet Jonas.　And he left them and departed."

It is obvious, that the words used on this latter
occasion by Christ, add nothing to the information
previously given concerning Jonah as a sign, and are
simply to be regarded as a new intimation and warning to the Jews of the important bearing of that sign
on their present circumstances, and the danger likely
to arise from their not giving heed to it.　But it is
equally obvious, that the information given on the
former occasion, when we combine together the accounts of the two evangelists, presents the sign in a *twofold* character to our view, and declares it to have had
an immediate and direct bearing on the Ninevites, as
well as an indirect and remote bearing on the Jews
of our Lord's time.　Jonah was first precisely such a
sign to the Ninevites as Christ was to the Jews; and,
secondly, Jonah was also a sign to the Jews, that they
might, by properly attending to it, be prepared for
understanding and receiving the things concerning
Christ.　The matter must be contemplated in both of
its aspects to be fully understood.

1. In what respect, then, was Jonah a sign to the
Ninevites?　It could not be as a prophet that he was
so designated ; for though the word *sign* is used with
considerable latitude in Scripture, yet it always de-

notes, when applied as here to the manifestations of
Godhead, something of the nature of a prodigy, an
extraordinary and undoubted operation of the hand
of God; and it must, therefore, have been meant to
be understood of Jonah, not simply as the Lord's
prophet to the Ninevites, but as himself a wonder in
the earth; being one who had, in a manner, tasted
of death, and yet had not seen corruption—who had
been sent into Sheol because of sin, and now again
returned to witness for righteousness among the
living, and show them the way of salvation. What
could more fitly deserve the name of a sign? Let us
mark the singular properties that belonged to it. It
was, first of all, wrought in secret, in the lower parts
of the earth—a work of God in a mystery; and, if
the Ninevites had chosen to treat the appearance of
Jonah among them with indifference and contempt,
no suspicion probably would ever have entered their
minds, at least no certain information would have
reached them, of the wonderful experience through
which he had passed. Then, it was a sign which for
Jonah himself was of a most humiliating nature; it
had marked him out as peculiarly the object of divine
resentment on account of sin, even to his being driven
forth as an outcast from God and man into the lowest
depths of abasement and distress; so that he had
himself occasion to be ashamed, rather than to boast
of what had happened; and the Ninevites—if, on
hearing the marvellous story, they had been disposed
to find an excuse for neglecting the message brought

to them—might have turned round on Jonah with
the taunt: " Physician, heal thyself ; thou who hast
so recently gone astray, and hast borne the just
wages of thy sin, art thou the man to come and cry
against us about transgression ?   Or are we to look to
thee for help, who hast proved so helpless for thyself ?"

But if, on the other hand, those Ninevites should
be actuated by a different spirit—if, on the voice of
this stranger being heard in their streets proclaiming
the speedy approach of God's judgment for sin, they
should incline their ear, and should inquire and learn
if so singular a messenger had any peculiar claims on
their confidence and respect, then what sign could
have been conceived so remarkably fitted to arrest
their attention, and enforce upon their minds the call
to repent?   For no sooner could they turn their
thoughts in this direction, than they should find that
the man who rung so unwelcome a message in their
ears, was in his own person a witness of the most
marvellous kind of God's purpose to be avenged of
sin, and specially to visit *them* in judgment for their
aggravated transgressions.   They would find that
the burden of their guilt and doom, when concealed
in his own bosom, instead of being proclaimed, as it
should have been, in the streets of Nineveh, had
rendered him an alien and an outcast from the land
of the living.   And now, when restored as from the
dead by an unprecedented display of divine power
and goodness, that he might go and charge it without
reserve upon themselves, what room any longer re-

mained for indifference or delay?   Or, if they should
agree to slight such an ambassador—what swift destruction might certainly be expected to alight on
their devoted heads?

Such thoughts would naturally arise even on the
first consideration of the matter; but there was
another thought still, which on further consideration
and deeper reflection could scarcely fail to impress
itself on the minds of the Ninevites. For Jonah,
who had formerly received into his bosom the wages
of transgression, was now a recovered victim—recovered even from the jaws of death and the regions
of corruption—and in his present condition he bore
no less striking evidence to the gracious and placable,
than in his past experience he had done to the holy
and righteous, character of God. As a sign, therefore, from God to the Ninevites, its full import could
only be read aright if they proceeded to reason thus
with themselves :—" There is here a token of good
bound up with the evil; this man's appearance is
the harbinger of hope to us, as well as the just
ground of fear and alarm. When we think of what
he has experienced, we should be of all men the
most foolish and reckless if we trifled with his message; but when we see him living and speaking in
the midst of us, we are taught not to despair at the
severity of its denunciations. The prophet has himself been dead and become alive again, lost and
again found; for what end, but that through his mercy
we might also obtain mercy, and that his restored

life might be the means of saving us from destruction !"

But are we quite certain that the Lord intended the Ninevites should thus become acquainted with what had previously befallen Jonah, and the precise character in which he now appeared? Unquestionably if Jonah, in respect to that portion of his history, was appointed to be a sign to the Ninevites; then, as such, the thing wrought must have been open at least to their inquiries, and capable of being ascertained, so as to produce its due effect upon their minds. If it *must* still have remained in concealment, however it might have served as a sign to others, it could not possibly have been a sign to the people of Nineveh. We therefore conclude, with perfect confidence, that God must have designed that they should inquire into the history of his messenger to them, and should obtain the requisite information concerning the remarkable dealings of God toward him. Nor, if we glance at the result of his embassy, can we entertain the slightest doubt that they became acquainted with what was past, and that the knowledge of it formed their chief motive for attending to the message proclaimed in their hearing. For is it to be imagined that the people of Nineveh, not rude and ignorant barbarians, but men whose minds were sharpened by the most extensive commerce, and many of whom lived in the highest luxury and refinement —is it for one moment to be imagined that they would be startled from their security, filled with consternation, brought to fasting and repentance, on the mere cry of impending ruin raised by a stranger, of whom they were totally ignorant, and who, for aught they knew, might only be uttering the dreams of his own excited fancy? By all the laws that are known to regulate human belief and conduct, we are not only warranted, but compelled to suppose, that, before such a result was attained, the most searching investigations had been made regarding the credibility of him who uttered the cry, and his claims on their confidence and regard. It was not simply the prophetic denunciation he uttered, but this recommended and enforced by the wonderful character of the sign which the prophet displayed before their eyes in his own person, that struck such astonishment and awe into the hearts of the people, and brought them, in contrition, and fear, and hope, to supplicate the mercy of God. With such a witness among them of the righteousness, the awful severity, and saving power of God, they felt that they durst not trifle with the word of threatening addressed to them.

Let us pause here for a moment to contemplate the wonder-working hand of God, and mark with what infinite skill it contrives to make all things redound to the glory of his name. It was the very things which befell Jonah, as the fruit and consequence of his backsliding, that fitted him to do the work of a successful ambassador to Nineveh. Had he gone on the first intimation, before his descent into the mighty deep, he would have wanted the most essential qualification for gaining the ear of the men of Nineveh, and arousing their consciences to a sense of their guilt and danger; he might have preached the same word of warning, but, in all probability, he would have preached in vain. And so God, in a manifold variety of ways, is ever manifesting his power to convert what is in itself evil into an instrument of good; from the eater he brings forth meat; and obtains means and instruments of blessing to his Church even from the dear-bought spoils of backsliding and correction. How many a successful combatant in the Lord's spiritual warfare has, like Saul the persecutor, derived his peculiar vantage-ground, and some of his most powerful weapons of assault, from his earlier experience in the ranks of the enemy! Saints too, like David or Peter, who have been permitted for a time to fall before temptation, and have thereby caused others to stumble or blaspheme, have still, by the very breaking of their bones, and their more lively and earnest grasp of the consolations of the gospel, become pre-eminently qualified for reviving the downcast, and strengthening tempted and troubled souls. To choose a course of evil for the ulterior good to which it may be rendered subservient, is a policy which can only have the devil for its author; but, from the evil already done, to extract an instrument or an occasion against the interests of the kingdom of darkness, is one of the most triumphant displays of the superabounding grace and manifold wisdom of God.

2. We have thus seen in what sense Jonah was a sign to the Ninevites. But his being a sign to them was no reason why he might not also be a sign to others, and in particular to the generation among whom our Lord exercised his personal ministry. It was characteristic of all the religious institutions and the dispensations of Providence, which were intended to speak to gospel times, that they had an end to serve for the time then present, as well as lessons of instruction to convey to a more distant age. The design of their appointment was to symbolize or embody truths, which were needed for those who lived in the earlier ages of the Church, and, at the same time, to typify things to come ; that is, to give promise of other things still future, in which the same truths should receive a higher manifestation, when the kingdom of God should have reached another and more advanced stage of development. And as Christ and the affairs of his everlasting kingdom were the grand and ultimate things to which, from the first, the divine administration pointed, so the determinate counsel and foreknowledge of God peculiarly showed itself in the times that are past, by arranging all in the institutions of worship and the events of life, with a view to their forming the most correct image of the greater things to come, and the most suitable preparation for their appearance. Hence, Jonah's being a sign (an embodied lesson or living symbol) to the Ninevites, not only did not hinder, but might rather peculiarly fit him for being also a

sign to a future generation of his own countrymen in respect to the history of Christ's work and kingdom; and as this last was the grand and ultimate object in the eye of God, there may have been—or, we should rather say, there doubtless *were*—things connected with this portion of the history of Jonah, of which the full meaning could not be discerned, nor the entire mystery solved, till the whole was seen in the light of Christ's finished undertaking.*

When our Lord took occasion to point to Jonah as a sign for the generation among whom he lived, it was, as we have seen, in reply to a solicitation on the part of some Scribes and Pharisees, that he would show them "a sign from heaven." This request, it will be remembered, was made at a pretty advanced stage of our Lord's earthly ministry—after multitudes of the most astonishing wonders and indubitable proofs of divine working had been exhibited by him in open day, and through many districts of the country. So that, by demanding a further sign, and, as contrasted with these, one that might appropriately be denominated a sign from heaven, they must have intended to seek, preparatory to their owning his claims as Messiah, some glorious display of the divine majesty upon him—such, perhaps, as the Shechinah of old, or the lustre that shone from the face of Moses, which, they imagined, could not be withheld from him if he were the Messiah, and which, if given, would at

* See the proof given of these general principles in the first volume of my *Typology*, Part I.

once dispel their doubts of the truth of his pretensions.

It was not possible that a request proceeding from
such a state of mind could meet with a favourable reception from Christ. In making it they were dispa-
raging the testimony raised in behalf of his Messiahship by all the mighty works which he had already
performed—the very works which ancient prophecy
had indicated should mark his footsteps upon earth.
They at once showed themselves to be labouring under
the most obdurate blindness, in slighting the signs
which in such great numbers had already proceeded
from his hand, and were guilty of intolerable pre-
sumption in prescribing the *kind* of sign which alone
they would deem entitled to their belief. Not only
so, but such a manifestation of glory as they were evidently bent on witnessing, would have been altogether
unsuited to the state of humiliation which became
him when travailing in pain for the world's redemption; and the very desire after it betrayed on their
part an unpreparedness of heart, a blindness and
alienation of mind, in respect to that spiritual glory
which shone from the faultless purity of his character,
and his execution of the work given him to do.
Christ, therefore, could plainly give no countenance
to their request. His answer must have possessed
the character of a rebuke—not of an encouragement;
and to suppose, as is commonly done, that in his reference to Jonah having been so long in the fish's
belly, and his own confinement for a like period in

the bowels of the earth, he pointed especially to the
safe deliverance in the one case, and the glorious resurrection in the other, as what might in the fullest
sense be considered a sign from heaven, is to give a
turn to the answer quite unsuited to the occasion.
Had such been the purport of our Lord's allusion and
reply, he would have substantially granted what they
sought.   " One sign only," he would in that case have
promised, to use the language of Calvin, " but that
as good as all: with this alone let them be content,
that as Jonas, after having escaped from the depths
of the sea, preached to the Ninevites, so they also
should hear the voice of the prophet raised from the
dead."

It is not to Jonah's safe deliverance from the belly
of the fish, and afterwards doing the work of a prophet, but simply to the fact of his *being* there before
going to Nineveh, that our Lord specially alludes.
Nor is it to his own resurrection from the dead, after
having been confined for a certain period in its gloomy
mansions, and resuming his work of mediatorial
agency, that he properly points in reference to himself.   He speaks only of his appointed descent into
the lower parts of the earth, as a movement to be
made by him precisely in the opposite direction to
that on which *their* expectations were turned.   " A
sign from heaven !" he virtually says to them, " will
nothing but that satisfy you that I am the Messiah
foretold by the prophets, and as such entitled to your
homage and regard ?   Will you receive no messenger

of heaven but one who comes to you recommended
by a blaze of supernatural glory, and arrayed in somewhat of the splendour of divine majesty? Your
own scriptures, if read aright, might teach you another
lesson, and put to shame your incredulity. Jonah,
whom you justly reverence as a true prophet, and who
was received in that character even by a heathen city,
carried with him thither no such attestations as you
expect from me; so far from it, he had but newly
escaped from that " belly of hell" to which divine
justice had sent him for the punishment of sin; yet
the Ninevites listened to his preaching, wisely looking
more to the truth of his message than to the circumstances of dishonour attending his history. And I—
so completely do ye misunderstand the nature of my
mission, and miscalculate regarding the circumstances
that are to mark its execution—must pass through a
similar, though still deeper, process of humiliation
than Jonah. The signs which are to discover themselves in me are to grow darker and not brighter;
they are to be derived, not from the heavens above,
but from the depths beneath—from the very chambers of the dead; yet am I not less on that account
the ambassador of heaven—nay, surpassing Jonah in
the depth of my humiliation, I still more surpass him
in the dignity of my character; and the inhabitants
of the heathen city, which repented at his preaching,
will assuredly rise up in judgment to condemn the
impenitence of this generation."

This, we conceive, is the purport of our Lord's

answer, and the precise object of his reference to Jonah. He meant to tell them, that they were looking in the wrong direction for an undoubted seal of his divine commission; and that the circumstances in which he appeared, and the nature of the work to which he was bound, required that he should bear upon him the signs, not of heavenly splendour, but of profound humiliation. Any other sign—any sign such as they expected—would have been a false one; it would have given a wrong impression of his character and work, and served to encourage them in the carnal views they cherished respecting the Messiah. He had no want of signs, in the proper sense, to manifest who and what he was; but they were signs which did not so much distinguish his person as reveal his character and work; and when so many wonders of a sanatory and restorative kind had proceeded from his hand, all proclaiming as with a voice from heaven what a blessed work of healing and recovery he had come to do among men, he justly charged them with hypocrisy in not being able to discern the signs of the times, and answered their expectations of a sign from heaven by pledging them a countersign from the heart of the earth.

Then, in the parallel case appealed to, what a striking identity of principle did it present to that of our Lord, notwithstanding the incidental and formal diversities that appeared between them! In both alike, a prophet sent to call a people to repentance— yet that prophet himself appearing in a low and

friendless condition—nay, bearing in such a sense the
burden of sin as to receive on account of it the awful
visitations of divine wrath, given over to death, and
only brought back again by the peculiar operation of
God—yet all ordered so, as, when rightly considered,
not to damage, but incalculably to promote the end
in view! In so many particulars do we perceive
here that oneness of principle pervading the two
cases, which ever constitutes the real connexion between type and antitype. And even some of the
non-essential circumstances of the type—such as the
preservation of Jonah in a sort of tomb under the
earth, rather than any other way; his detention there
for the period precisely of three days and three
nights, or a part of these according to the eastern
mode of computation; and the very language he used
so literally descriptive of a state of death—these
merely circumstantial things in the case of Jonah,
which look, perhaps, somewhat strange or capricious
when viewed simply with reference to himself, have
only to be seen in relation to their ultimate design to
acquire light and meaning. They were so many
distinctive marks in the outward shell of the transaction, to enable the contemporaries of Jesus the more
easily to read its hidden import, and descry the more
essential lines of resemblance between his case and
that of the prophet of Gath-hepher. Happy, if they
had but received the instruction, which divine wisdom
had thus so long before prepared for their good!
But pride with most of them still bore the ascendant.

They would not stoop to regard themselves in the condition of Nineveh, as a people needing to repent, or requiring a Messiah who had aught to do with punishment and death; and so, what should have proved a guiding star to the Saviour, stands only as a pillar of witness to condemn their incurable folly and perverseness.

It were well, however, if those persons stood alone in their condemnation. But the error into which they fell, was the natural offspring of a carnal heart; and under other forms it is constantly repeating itself. There are two different ways especially, in which it is often appearing in present times.

1. It appears in those hearers of the gospel, who, instead of looking to the message itself, and applying their hearts faithfully to the things which it sets before them, fix their eye upon something connected with the bearers of it, which differs from their ideas of what is right and proper, and which they deem sufficient to justify them in neglecting the very substance of the message. The doctrines pressed upon their acceptance may be ever so well fitted to command their reverence, and the duties to which they are called may be of the gravest importance and connected with the most pressing obligations—but they have some exception to take against the instrument through which the whole is conveyed to them, or the manner in which it is delivered; and on that account they hold themselves excused from taking much thought about the matter. It is not enough

for them, that divine truth descends from heaven to present herself to their embrace; she must come attired in the precise form and dress which they conceive suited to her lofty origin, otherwise they will not so much as give her a respectful audience. It is not enough that the call to repent, and to do things meet for repentance, is heard by them, and inwardly responded to by the voice of conscience, as well as enforced by what is most fitted to move and influence the heart—if it is not also accredited to their outward senses by becoming signs of honour and authority, they will leave the demand unsatisfied! What preposterous folly in reasonable creatures! As if the shell were more than the kernel it contains —or the voice of Heaven were only to be listened to when it falls upon the ear with attractive and winning sounds! Surely when that voice cries, the first and grand consideration should always be, *what* does it cry—not how, with what peculiar tone, or with what attendant circumstances! Let it only meet with a patient hearing, and due regard be paid to the substance of the message, and there will be no occasion to doubt either the nature of the communication, or the quarter from which it proceeds. " If any man *will do* his will, he shall know of the doctrine whether it be of God."

2. It is but another form of the same fundamental error which appears sometimes in a total rejection of the claims of the gospel, or in a disavowal of some of its essential parts—because not possessing a certain

kind or amount of evidence, which is pre-supposed
to have been necessary if it had been truly of God.
The scribes and Pharisees would not own Christ as
a divine messenger on account of the supernatural
signs he actually showed, but they professed their
readiness to do so if he produced a sign of a different
kind—a sign from heaven. The mass of the people
would not believe in him because he had saved so
many from mortal disease and death during the period
of his active ministry; but if he could have saved
himself from the doom of impending destruction when
hanging on the cross, then they would have believed.
So the wayward will of man, in its mad controversy
with the will of God, is always ready to take exception against the means he graciously employs to overcome it, and pitches upon something else, something
of its own, which alone it will regard as satisfactory.
It has the audacity of prescribing to its Maker, and,
instead of humbly sitting down to weigh the grounds
on which he challenges its belief and obedience, it
presumptuously insists upon certain terms of its own
as indispensable. How could Jesus of Nazareth have
been so generally rejected by his own countrymen (certain unbelievers have asked with the view of finding
some colour for their unbelief), if he had been manifested among them as the Son of God with power?
And if salvation really depended upon the reception
of the truths of his gospel, how could it have been
confined by a merciful God to so small a portion of
mankind, and not communicated to the world at

large? Others, again, who would not dispense with the whole gospel, but only with some of its more peculiar doctrines or observances, conceive themselves warranted in rejecting these, because they are not to be found in such portions of Scripture, or do not stand out in so unequivocal and prominent a form as might have been anticipated. But who art thou that wouldst dictate to God how he is to disclose his will, or with what degrees of light and conviction he is to accompany it? The question for thee to consider, in regard to any doctrine revealed or any duty imposed in the word of his gospel, is simply, whether such may not be ascertained to be the mind and will of God by all who are honestly desirous of knowing it. Is there not light clear and satisfactory enough to determine the convictions and direct the course of every one who looks with a single eye to what is before him? It never was God's intention, in the communication of his truth to man, to render all evasion impossible on the part of such as are inwardly bent on shunning the obligations it brings. Persons of this description will always be able to find some plausible, though shallow, pretext on which to excuse their unwillingness. But such persons, on the other hand, as walk humbly with their God, and are content to look at the signs which he himself has furnished for their guidance and instruction, will find nothing to be wanting that an enlightened faith can require. " For the ways of the Lord are right, and

the just shall walk therein; but the transgressors
shall fall therein."

All this, however, it must be remembered, has respect only to one aspect of the Jonah-like sign which
our Lord's history was to present to the men of his
generation—the descent on his part into the bowels
of the earth, and on theirs the *necessity* of repenting
and turning to the Lord. This was the peculiar
aspect which the occasions arising in Christ's ministry,
and the general character of the times, naturally led
him to bring out most distinctly into view. It is also
for the world at large the most important. For, in
the work of Christ, all may be said to hinge upon
his death; the centre is there, and without it nothing
as regards salvation is accomplished, either in the
scheme of God or in the experience of man. Apart
from this death, the call to repent loses its mightiest
argument—the exhibition of God's avenging righteousness in the awful sacrifice of the cross; and even
if repentance could be exercised, the most fervent and
sincere, it would still be of no avail for the sinner's
restoration to peace and blessing, as without the death
of Christ there were no solid ground for him on which
to make an acceptable return to God. On this account doubtless it was, that not only, as when a
sign from heaven was asked, were suitable occasions
readily embraced, but other occasions also, and such
as might even seem scarcely suitable ones, were stu-
diously sought to direct men's thoughts to the death

of Jesus, as the event out of which the grand results were to grow for his Church and kingdom. As when, for example, amid the glories of the transfiguration, Moses and Elias made it, though apparently out of place at such a time, the one topic of their discourse with him—" they spake of the decease which he should accomplish at Jerusalem." Or when, after expelling, on the first occasion, the buyers and sellers from the temple, and a sign being demanded for his authority to interfere in such a manner with the house of God, he said, " Destroy this temple, and in three days I will raise it up again,"—pointing to the death and resurrection of his own body. Or, once more, when, in the brief discourse that followed the presentation of certain Grecians before him, as recorded in the 12th chapter of John's gospel, he not only began by declaring, " Verily, verily, I say unto you, Except a corn of wheat fall into the ground and die, it abideth alone ; but if it die, it bringeth forth much fruit ;" but afterwards again reverted to the subject in these peculiar and somewhat enigmatical words : " And I, if I be lifted up, will draw all men to me." Such allusions beforehand to the death of Jesus, can only be accounted for on the supposition of its holding such a pre-eminent place, that it was, so to speak, the grand centre to which every thing previously tended, and out of which the issues of God's kingdom were afterwards to unfold themselves.

But the other aspect of the sign, its bearing upon

the *encouragement* to repent, and its connexion more
immediately with the return of Christ from " the heart
of the earth," his rising again from the dead and as-
cending to the right hand of God—this, though not
specially noticed by our Lord in the passages formerly
referred to, was certainly not intended to be left out
of view. It is plainly included in his being a sign to
the Jews such as Jonah was to the Ninevites. And
though his pointing to that sign, with the assurance
that no other would be given them, might at first seem
to betoken only trouble and disaster to his mission,
yet the more thoughtful and discerning minds would
not fail to discover, on further reflection, that there
was also couched under it a promise of encouragement and success far beyond any thing that had
hitherto appeared. He was to become to the world the
sign that Jonah was to Nineveh only when he entered
upon the resurrection-life, and in his name repentance
and remission of sins were preached to the people.
And hence the great stress laid upon the fact of the
resurrection by the first heralds of the gospel, and the
wonderful effect produced by it upon those who heard
them, not simply because of the proof it afforded of
the truth of Christ's pretensions to be the Son of God,
but also and still more from the impressive attestation,
the living witness it gave of the placability of God,
and of the holy earnestness of his desire that sinners
would repent and live. Precisely as in the case of
Jonah, though in a manner unspeakably more solemn
and affecting, the things that had befallen Jesus, and

the condition in which he now presented himself through his ambassadors to the people, were seen to be a most singular and magnificent provision of love on the part of God to reach their consciences, and to avert, ere it might be too late, the doom of condemnation which divine justice had suspended over their heads.

With this resemblance between the two cases, there was, of course, a real and fundamental difference. Jonah's descent into the deep, and his return again to the land of the living, could at the most operate but as the means of moral suasion upon the minds of the Ninevites; and even in that respect it fell far short of what is contained in the death and resurrection of Christ. But in the case of Christ this instrumental power carries along with it, and is grounded upon, an inherent efficacious virtue. He actually did what Jonah could not be said to do, except in a kind of figurative and shadowy sense—bore, in his treatment as an outcast, the burden of their guilt and condemnation whom he was sent to save, and in his resurrection from the dead, became for them the seed-corn of a glorious harvest—the wellspring of a new and eternal life like his own. Jesus, dying and descending into the chambers of death, is the sign of God's judgment flaming out against the transgressions of the guilty; the same Jesus risen and glorified is the sign of mercy rejoicing against judgment, and ready to flow out in streams of life and blessing to the penitent. And the voice that now emphatically comes to awakened souls from the risen and exalted Saviour, speaks in such a strain as this to them, "Believe and live; behold in me the infallible proof that the justice of the Father is satisfied for sin, and that he is willing to bestow everlasting life on all who will enter through repentance and faith into the fellowship of what I have experienced and done; and be assured and doubt not, that wherever the word of salvation is now sent, it is sent to bless you in turning every one of you away from his iniquities."

CHAPTER VI

THE sojourn of Jonah for a time in the deep waters,
and his singular experience there, having been mainly
designed to prepare him for doing aright the work of
the Lord's ambassador to Nineveh, he was no sooner
restored to the dry land, than " the word of the Lord
came to him the second time, saying, Arise, go unto
Nineveh, that great city, and preach unto it the
preaching that I bid thee;" or, more exactly, "proclaim to it the proclamation that I speak to thee."
" So Jonah arose, and went to Nineveh, according to
the word of the Lord. And Jonah began to enter
into the city a day's journey, and he cried, and said,
Yet forty days, and Nineveh shall be overthrown."

Two things strike us here. The first is, the inde-
terminate form of the commission as now delivered
on this second occasion to Jonah. When formerly
issued, the specific object was at the same time declared for which he was to repair to Nineveh. He

was to cry against it, because its wickedness had come up before the Lord. But now he must go without any definite instruction as to the precise end in view, with a readiness merely to proclaim whatever word the Lord might be pleased to put into his mouth. This, no doubt, was done for the purpose of more clearly exhibiting how much he now possessed of the spirit of unconditional obedience, and how freely he yielded himself as an instrument of service to God. Not by the substance only, but also by the very form of the commission he bore, he must go forth breathing the sentiment, " I delight to do thy will, O my God! thy law is within my heart."

The other peculiarity here is, that when the general commission given to Jonah before his setting out for Nineveh, assumes on his arrival there a more express and definite form, it presents a considerably severer aspect than it originally wore. It is no longer a cry against the sins and abominations prevailing in Nineveh, but an authoritative and explicit announcement, that the ruin of the city was at hand: " Yet forty days, and Nineveh shall be overthrown." Such was the word actually put into the mouth of Jonah; and the marked difference between it and the one formerly given, as it cannot have been unintentional, neither is it to be regarded as of slight importance.*

---

* It is strange that this difference should be so entirely overlooked by commentators, and still more strange, that Matthew Henry should so expressly affirm, that the first and second message were entirely the same!

Why precisely forty days should have been fixed as the ultimate period of Nineveh's existence as a city, and by what means the Lord purposed at the close of that period to overthrow it, we need not busy ourselves in attempting to conjecture, as these are points which it is impossible for us, in the absence of all information, to ascertain.   But the fact of the message having passed, during the interval between the two communications, from a mere expostulation on account of sin, into the proclamation of an immediately impending doom, was plainly intended to mark the downward and darkening progress of things. The people with whom the prophet has to transact, are now in far more dangerous and desperate circumstances than before; they have reached within a few steps of the awful gulf, toward which their career of sin has long been precipitating them; and Jonah has but the melancholy, and it might be, in the circumstances, perilous task, of ringing in their ears a little beforehand the sound of the approaching calamity.

An important and salutary lesson was here conveyed to Jonah, and through him to every servant of heaven. For, how manifest had the sin and folly now become of delaying to execute the work of God, on account of the difficulties and troubles which at the first seemed to hang around it! These, it was found in this case, became not less but greater by the delay, and so it will ever be found. He who has a task from God to discharge for the good of others, if he would not aggravate the burden to himself, let him apply promptly to the performance of what is required at his hands; for, if the records of all experience were searched, there is nothing in respect to which they would be found to give a more clear and uniform testimony than this, that apart altogether from the recompenses of evil, which are ever ready to chastise a spirit of disobedience, incomparably the wisest and happiest course is to fulfil the behests of duty at the proper time, as well as in the appointed way.

But a lesson still more impressive and startling was doubtless also intended, by the circumstance in question, to be conveyed to the Ninevites themselves. That a prophet should have been first commissioned to go from Israel and cry against their sins, because of their enormous wickedness; and then, after the delay occasioned by the prophet's own backwardness to fulfil the appointment, that he should on the renewal of the commission have been instructed to proclaim the sure destruction of Nineveh itself in the short space of forty days—this was certainly an appalling change for them. It indicated how rapidly the measure of their iniquities had meanwhile been filling up, and how near the forbearance of heaven had come to its termination. Nor can we reasonably doubt, that the change from the first to the second commission was perfectly known to the people of Nineveh before the message of the prophet had produced its due effect upon their minds. In the brief notice that is given of his labours at Nineveh, we have manifestly nothing more than the substance of his preaching, without the circumstantials, which were still essentially connected with its extraordinary success. And as we have already shown that the people must, either from spontaneous communications on Jonah's part, or, as is more probable, in answer to their own anxious inquiries, have become acquainted with his previous history, in order to his being such a *sign* to them as God's purpose required, we can have the less difficulty in conceiving that not only the message ultimately delivered, but that also which *should* have been delivered at an earlier stage of the history, were alike made known to them.

It is true, the people *might* have remained ignorant of any thing either in the past history of Jonah himself, or in the comparative stringency of the two messages he had received concerning them. They might have treated his appearance and his cry in their streets with supercilious scorn, as the act of a dreaming enthusiast; or, looking to their own lofty walls and numerous defences, they might have asked with an incredulous sneer, where the enemy was to be found that in forty days could level these with the dust? But it is to the credit of the Ninevites that they gave a different reception to this message of heaven. They neither treated the message itself with mockery, nor the bearer of it with violence and insult, but brought their minds with one accord to consider the peculiar circumstances in which they were placed, and to know the whole of the matter. Let us try to picture to our minds the wonderful phenomenon that then presented itself in Nineveh. A stranger of foreign mien appears of a sudden in the streets, crying aloud, " Yet forty days, and Nineveh shall be overthrown." He passes on from one portion of the city to another, and still the same cry is heard from his lips; he has no other word. Who and what is he? Is it a madman who thus speaks, or a mocker, who delights to "scatter firebrands, arrows, and death?" His intelligent and sober aspect forbids the supposition; he bears himself as a man deeply in earnest, and alive to the awful importance of the work he has in hand; and the very oneness of the message he delivers—that he has just this solitary message to proclaim—seems to betoken all the more an assured conviction of the truth and certainty of *it*. The busy crowd is by and by arrested; a solemn awe steals over the minds of the people; they press around the preacher to know whence he is, and why he utters such an ominous cry in their streets; and learning, as they now do, that so far from lightly speaking evil concerning them, he had already at the hazard of his life shrunk from executing the charge committed to him—shrunk from executing it when it simply required him to testify against the sins that prevailed in the midst of them—that he had been cast out for his wilful reluctance into the mighty deep, and miraculously restored only that he might be sent forth anew, with a still more severe and urgent message, to utter the loud cry they now heard of approaching destruction:—learning all this concerning Jonah and his burden, how solemn and perilous must their situation have appeared in their eyes! Though personally a stranger to them, this man's fortunes, it seems, have yet been most intimately bound up with theirs; he has undergone wonderful and unheard-of things on their account. And the tide of divine wrath, all unconsciously to them, has been rising higher and higher around them, till it has left them as prisoners of justice on an isolated point, ready to be swept away into the devouring gulf! What grounds for serious consideration and alarm!*

A spirit of reckless levity and unbelief might still have led the people to treat all with indifference, and to add to their other sins by rejecting the Lord's messenger as a false witness, and one that sought to trouble them with groundless fears. But a different spirit happily prevailed; and, regarding themselves as standing on the verge of ruin, they now presented the example of a people effectually roused from their spiritual slumber, and applying in earnest to the work of reformation. " So the people of Nineveh believed God,

* It is, of course, quite conceivable, and by no means unlikely, that certain events or circumstances in providence may have concurred with the appearance and preaching of Jonah to enforce and deepen this impression upon the minds of the people. There may have been accompanying signs of terror in the elements of nature, threatening an earthquake; or in the expected assault of some hostile neighbours, such as might give to the doom announced by the prophet the aspect of a near and pressing reality. But, whatever probability there may be in such conjectures, they still belong to the region of conjecture, and are not to be much accounted of. We have to do simply with the known facts of the case.

and proclaimed a fast, and put on sackcloth, from the greatest of them even to the least of them. For word came unto the king of Nineveh, and he arose from his throne, and he laid his robe from him, and covered him with sackcloth, and sat in ashes. And he caused it to be proclaimed and published through Nineveh by the decree of the king and his nobles, saying, Let neither man nor beast, herd nor flock, taste any thing: let them not feed, nor drink water: but let man and beast be covered with sackcloth, and cry mightily unto God: yea, let them turn every one from his evil way, and from the violence that is in their hands. Who can tell if God will turn and repent, and turn away from his fierce anger, that we perish not?"

1. In these words, considered as a description of sincere and genuine repentance, we have to note, *first,* the awakened and heartfelt concern which pervaded the people. All classes shared in it, and those now took the lead in expressing their convictions of guilt and danger, whose situation invested them with the greatest responsibility. The king and nobles of Nineveh were not ashamed to own themselves believers in the word of God, and afraid of suffering the inflictions of his displeasure; but, convinced themselves of the greatness of the emergency, they endeavoured to arouse others to the same, not by any external compulsion, but by openly accrediting, on their authority, the truthfulness of the prophet's testimony, and calling upon the people to meet the evil that threatened them in a becoming spirit. Happy for Nineveh at such a season

that her rulers knew thus the time of their visitation! And happy must it be for any land, when those who occupy its highest places of power and influence are the foremost in confessing the truth of God, and acting suitably to its requirements! Unfortunately, it is rather the reverse of this which usually attracts our notice. The spirit of the gospel, instead of coming down from the higher places of the earth, recommended by all that is attractive and influential in society, has for the most part been left to work its way upward in the face of a counter spirit, nowhere so firmly seated and so vigorously put forth as in the palaces of the great. But whether among great or small, whenever the word of God really takes hold of the conscience, the first symptom always discovers itself in such a spirit of heartfelt concern as we find here, leading men to grapple in earnest with the things of God, and rendering it impossible for them any longer to trifle with interests so momentous, and dangers so pressing.

2. *Secondly*, The repentance at Nineveh was marked by a spirit of deep humiliation and abasement. This was manifested by a variety of outward actions, in accordance partly with the lively temperament of the people of the East, and partly also with the symbolical spirit which so deeply pervaded the religions of antiquity. Both circumstances naturally led the Ninevites to embody in external acts and corporeal gestures the pungent feelings that were experienced in their bosom. The clothing with sack-

cloth, therefore, sitting in ashes and fasting, in which
to some extent even the cattle were made to take
their share, in token of the felt urgency of the case,
is merely to be regarded as the sign—in their circumstances the natural and appropriate sign—of a deeply
humbled and prostrate heart.   Apart from this, such
things were not then, neither are they now, of any
worth in the sight of God, and hence are never enjoined in Scripture as in themselves ordinances of
God, having an inherent efficacy and value.   Appropriate forms they were, and nothing more, through
which the heart, pierced with convictions of sin, and
trembling for fear of God's judgments, might give
outward expression to what it felt within.   It was
still the state of heart itself on which God looked
with satisfaction—both then, when such external
forms were commonly resorted to, and now, when they
are as commonly laid aside.*

* Some even among Protestants (to say nothing of the cere-
monialists of Rome, and their semi-Protestant imitators) are
disposed to make an exception in favour of fasting, and to regard
it as in the proper sense an ordinance of God, and one still in
force.   Such persons can of course appeal to the practice of the
apostolic Church.   On more than one occasion we read of the disciples giving themselves to fasting; and in 1 Cor. vii. 5, St Paul,
according to the authorized version, exhorts believers at Corinth
in certain circumstances "rather to give themselves to fasting
and prayer."   The reading of this text is now universally regarded
as corrupt, and in the later editions of the original the word for
fasting is omitted.   In regard to the practice of the primitive
Church, it is neither set forth, nor can it properly be viewed, as
a rule; for it was evidently continued as a custom from former
times, just as the anointing of the sick in Mark vi. 13, and James

3. Again, the reformation at Nineveh discovered its genuineness by proper resolutions and purposes of amendment. The sorrow and regret that were felt for the past, gave rise to better counsels for the future; each one turned from his evil way, and from the violence that was in their hands. By this the Ninevites showed how well they had come to understand the character of God. They knew him to be no capricious and arbitrary being, but holy, just, and good— one who comes near to the execution of judgment

v. 14, the abstinence from blood, and observance of Jewish customs generally. But not even in the law of Moses (notwithstanding that fasting came to be much in use among the Jews), was there any command respecting fasting. The only thing approaching to it is the injunction on the people " to afflict their souls " on the day of atonement, which in later times was understood to require a corporeal fast, as in earlier ones it was very probably accompanied with the same. Hence the day itself was familiarly called *the fast.*—(Acts xxvii. 9.) Such corporeal abstinence was never properly enjoined; it is even plainly disparaged by the prophets (Isa. lviii. 3–6; Zech. vii. 5; Joel ii. 12, 13), on account of the strong tendency of the mind to substitute this mere bodily deprivation for internal compunction. And what our Lord says in Matt. vi. evidently points in the same direction; even when men did feel it proper to fast, they were still to anoint their heads, and not appear unto others to fast. Our Lord sought to call men away from the mere outward act to the humbled and contrite spirit, which alone was of any account in the sight of God. When persons find from experience that this spiritual effect may be best produced by the accompaniment of outward fasting, they are doubtless at liberty to follow the practice, though the danger will always require to be well guarded against of its degenerating into formalism, and feeding the spirit of self-righteousness. A judicious and sensible essay on this subject was lately published by Mr John Collyer Knight, London.

only as the righteous avenger of sin, and who must, therefore, regard all repentance as a mockery which stops short of a renunciation and abhorrence of the misdeeds which have provoked his displeasure. By turning from *their* misdeeds on this occasion, the Ninevites justified God as righteous for having come near to them, as he did, in the way of judgment; and virtually declared that they had no reason to expect the reversal of the doom but by entering on paths conformable to his holiness. What a reflection would it involve on the character of God for any one to think otherwise! God must first cease to be the Holy One and the Just, before he can recall the sentence of condemnation against transgressors, and make them partakers of blessing while they are still following the ways of unrighteousness—he must appear, if not directly the patron of sin, at least comparatively indifferent to the distinctions between right and wrong!

4. The last step in a true repentance—the return in faith and confidence to God—is also represented to have been taken by the Ninevites. Without this their repentance could certainly not have been complete; for as the essence of all sin consists in the spirit of independence and enmity it manifests in respect to God, so it is only when the soul has returned to seek repose and blessing in God, that the evil can be said to have ceased in its root. This return, we are led to understand, was made by the people of Nineveh, since they are said to have " cried mightily

to the Lord," and to have sought with one heart to obtain an interest in his favour and blessing ;—a procedure the more remarkable in their case, as, being naturally heathens, they had to break through the wall of long-established prejudices before they could make *any* approach to Jehovah. And remarkable still farther, when it is considered how narrow the ground was on which they had to stand for the exercise of hope and confidence toward God. For the word, which they are said to have believed, held out no promise of good ; it breathed only threatening and destruction ; it was with them now precisely as it had already been with Jonah when cast into the deep—the heavens seemed all so enveloped in darkness, that scarcely an opening remained for hope to enter. Without any *special* grounds of encouragement, they were obliged to betake themselves to merely general considerations. " Who can tell," they said, " but God will turn and repent, and turn away from his fierce anger, that we perish not ? We cannot plead this on the score of justice, neither can we ply his faithfulness with any specific assurance of mercy, given to meet the necessities of our case ; we have nothing to encourage us but the general character of God himself, as manifested in his dealings with men on earth. But still we have that, and the matter is not altogether hopeless. For why should God have sent his prophet to admonish us of sin, and foretell his approaching judgment, a prophet, too, who has himself been the subject of singular mercy and forbearance? If destruction alone had been his object, would he not rather have allowed us to sleep on in our sinfulness? And why, in particular, should these forty days have been made to run between our doom and our punishment? Surely this bespeaks some thought of mercy in God; it must have been meant to leave the door still open to us for forgiveness and peace."

So undoubtedly they reasoned, and, as the event proved, reasoned justly. Like men in earnest to be saved, they were determined to seize the present moment; and, in their manner of doing so, showed somewhat of that quickness of perception in apprehending grounds of forgiveness and hope, which had previously been manifested by Jonah himself in the hour of his extremity. Little as they had to warrant their confidence in God, that little, with faith, was sufficient. And, putting the whole together, we certainly have before us, in the case of the people of Nineveh, an example of sincere and genuine repentance. Their conduct on the occasion exhibited the usual marks and exercises of grace, which are the proper characteristics of such a repentance; and it received the indubitable seal of the divine approbation. For we are told, " God saw their works, that they turned from their evil way;" and our Lord pointed to them as a people who had in truth repented of sin and turned to God.

Possibly, however, certain thoughts may suggest themselves not altogether consistent with the view

now given; for if the Ninevites indeed broke off their
sins, and turned with one heart to the living God,
why, it may be asked, do we hear nothing of their
frequenting, as true worshippers, the temple of God
in Jerusalem? and why, in all the subsequent accounts presented to us of Nineveh, both in the history
of ancient Israel and in the prophets, do they constantly appear as a race of idolaters, maintaining a
rival interest with God's covenant people, and themselves, in process of time, visited with destruction, for
their intolerable pride, revelry, and lust?

There can be no question that the reformation
effected at Nineveh, through the instrumentality of
Jonah, was not perpetuated so as to impress a lasting
change on the character of the people, and it is possible that in comparatively few of them was it of that
high kind which endures unto life everlasting. Yet
we have no reason to suppose that there was an immediate or even very rapid return to the former state
of things. For, taking the visit of Jonah to have occurred about the middle of the reign of Jeroboam II.,
which is probably even later than the period of its
actual occurrence, the earliest notice we have subse-
quently of the Assyrian empire or people is at a distance of thirty or forty years, and consists simply of
the fact, that Pul, the king of Assyria, came up against
Menahem, king of Israel, and laid him under tribute;
but in what spirit this act of aggression was made, or
what it indicated morally respecting Assyria, we are
utterly ignorant. It is not till the invasion of Judah

by Sennacherib, in the reign of Hezekiah, that the
king and people of Nineveh appear in the attitude of
defiers of Jehovah, and as the representatives of the
world-power in its opposition to the kingdom and
glory of God. But this could scarcely have been less
than a century after the preaching of Jonah, leaving
ample room for an entire change meanwhile entering
into the moral condition of the people, as there seems
also to have sprung up a new spirit in the government and direction of its civil affairs—a spirit of
military ambition and conquest, of which no traces
exist in the earlier history of the kingdom. By the
period of Sennacherib's reign, not only had two entire
generations passed away since the memorable preaching of Jonah; but it is more than probable that, as
happened shortly after in Babylon, a new and more
warlike race had obtained the mastery of affairs at
Nineveh, so that no conclusion can be drawn thence
respecting the posture of things at the time now under
consideration.*

* No one who is at all read in ancient history needs to be
told of the sudden changes, and even entire revolutions, to which
the cities and empires of a remote antiquity were subject. The
revolution referred to above in the case of Babylon may
especially help us to understand, how easily the whole aspect of
affairs may have changed at Nineveh in a far shorter time than
that now supposed. Speaking of the Babylonians about 630
years before Christ, Heeren says, " A revolution then took place
in Asia, similar to that which Cyrus afterwards effected. A
nomad people, under the name of Chaldean, descending from the
mountains of Taurus and Caucasus, overwhelmed Southern Asia,
and made themselves masters of the Syrian and Babylonian

If these later notices of the Assyrian empire are not fitted to involve the reformation effected by Jonah in any doubt, neither certainly is the absence of any intimation of worshippers having come from Nineveh to Jerusalem. It was in the nature of things impossible, that persons at so great a distance, on the supposition of their being sincere converts to the knowledge and worship of Jehovah, should come in any considerable numbers to wait on him at Jerusalem. And it is doubtful how far this was required at the hands of any not actually incorporated with the seed of Jacob, and residing within the bounds of the land of Canaan. The whole economy and institutions of Moses were adapted to such; and those who might come to the knowledge of God, while incapable from their situation or distance of complying with the letter of the law, were left to follow such a course as seemed most accordant with the general spirit of its enactments. Hence no fault is found with Naaman the Syrian because he purposed to erect an altar in his native land, and call there upon

plains. Babylonia, which they captured, became the chief seat of their empire, and their king Nebuchadnezzar, by subduing Asia to the shores of the Mediterranean, earned his title to be ranked among the most famous of Asiatic conquerors." To this event the prophet Isaiah has been thought to point in chap. xxiii. 13, " Behold the land of the Chaldeans ; this people was not; Assyria founded it for them that dwelt in the wilderness ; " —*i. e.* as many understand it, the Chaldeans, who possessed Babylon, were not its original occupants, nor were they of ancient origin; the Assyrians in a manner founded and prepared it for them.

the name of the Lord.   Nor, at a much later period,
is the least doubt thrown upon the sincerity of the
homage paid to the infant Jesus by the eastern Magi,
or the worth of their testimony depreciated on account of their at once and for ever disappearing from
the scene of gospel history.   They had a special light
granted them from heaven, and their wisdom consisted in faithfully following its direction as far as it
carried them.   In like manner, the Ninevites in the
days of Jonah were placed for the time under a peculiar dispensation; it was their wisdom to have followed with ready alacrity the light of that dispensation; and our inability to lift the veil which scripture
has allowed to rest upon their future condition, or to
determine certain ulterior questions respecting them,
should on no account be turned into an occasion
for disputing the reality of their conversion, or
depreciating the character of the work wrought in
the midst of them.   They had for a time a supernatural light; they so used and rejoiced in that light
as to receive the benediction of God; and who are
we, that we should eye them with suspicion and
doubt?

The case of the Ninevites stands for all ages as a
memorable example how little instruction will suffice
when the heart is properly disposed to make a profitable use of it.   The light that shone upon them was
but a faint glimmering compared with the full blaze
of truth which now irradiates the world—and yet it
proved sufficient to bring them into the way of peace

and blessing. Would that the believing and earnest spirit, which then wrought so powerfully at Nineveh, did but pervade and rest upon the lands of the Bible now—what different fruits would appear from those which are commonly seen amongst men! Instead of seeking for excuses to cloak their indifference, or standing aloof under benumbing fears and doubts, as multitudes are wont to do, sinners would be every where seen awaking to spiritual life, and laying hold of the arm of God for salvation. Nineveh, alas! must still be to most but a witness to condemn in judgment, not an example to prompt and encourage their return to God. Yet seldom has God given a more unequivocal proof, than in his dealings with Nineveh, that he wills not the death of the sinner, but that the sinner should turn to him and live.

CHAPTER VII

THE intimation given in the book of Jonah regarding
the procedure of God toward Nineveh in the new circumstances in which it now stood, is delivered with
great simplicity, and as if no feeling of surprise should
have been occasioned by it: "And God saw their
works, that they turned from their evil way; and God
repented of the evil, that he had said that he would
do unto them; and he did it not." Important principles, however, are embodied in this statement, and
it will require to be viewed in more than one aspect.

1. It may be viewed, first of all, as the record
simply of a fact in providence; in which respect the
most direct lesson it furnishes is one of ample encouragement to the sincere penitent. When God sent
his messenger to Nineveh, the people were so ripe for
judgment, that a purpose of destruction, to take effect
in forty days, was the only word he could publish in
their hearing. But no sooner does he see the message

laid seriously to heart, and the people with one consent returning from sin to God, than the purpose of
destruction is recalled, the threatened doom is suspended, and Nineveh is still spared. Nothing could
more strikingly show the unwillingness of God to
execute vengeance, and the certainty with which every
true penitent may count upon finding an interest in his
pardoning mercy. He will rather expose his proceedings to the hazard of being misunderstood by shallow
and superficial men, than allow the penalty due to un-
forgiven sin to fall upon such as have turned in earnest
from its ruinous courses. What an assurance did the
world then receive that God is rich in mercy and plen-
teous in redemption! He came down, in a manner, to
its most public theatre, and in deeds more expressive
than words, proclaimed, "Look unto me, all the ends
of the earth, and be ye saved." "Let the wicked forsake his way, and the unrighteous man his thoughts,
and let him return unto the Lord, and he will have
mercy upon him; and to our God, for he will abundantly pardon."

At the same time, it is not to be overlooked, that
along with this direct lesson, and in close connection
with it, there was furnished through the Lord's dealing with Nineveh an indirect warning and instruction
to those who persist in impenitence and sin. Viewed,
for example, in relation to Israel, the prophet's own
people, the sparing of Nineveh on account of its repentance was an anticipatory vindication of God in regard to the severe course he was purposing to adopt

in respect to those children of the covenant; it was like the laying down of a solemn pledge before the world, that the desolating judgment, when it *should* alight on them, must be ascribed, not to any harshness in his character, but solely to their own incorrigible and hardened impenitence. They had claims on his compassion which Nineveh had not; and their destruction in spite of these, viewed in connection with the sparing of that heathen city, was an unanswerable proof of their inexcusable folly and perverseness. They were thus seen to be emphatically the authors of their own ruin. And the same end substantially is still served by the preservation of the repenting Ninevites; it stands as a perpetual witness against the lost, throwing the blame of their perdition entirely upon their own heads; so that God shall be justified when he speaks concerning them, and clear when he is judged.

2. But the sparing of Nineveh on its repentance may be viewed, *secondly*, in connection with the word spoken to it by Jonah in the name of the Lord—the word announcing its coming doom, in which respect it serves to throw light on the threatenings of God generally. The sharp contrast between what God had spoken and what he actually did—his declaring without reserve a purpose of evil, and still abstaining from the execution of the purpose, was wont to be explained by drawing a distinction between God's secret and his revealed will—between his *real* intention or decree, which remains, like himself, fixed and immutable,

and his *declared* intention, which may vary with the changeful conditions of those to whom it refers. But such a mode of representation, however it may accord with the essential truth of things, wears an unhappy aspect; and even when most carefully guarded and defined, can scarcely be separated from an appearance of insincerity on the part of God, as if he could speak otherwise than he really thinks in his heart. It is far more conformable to our natural feelings, and consistent with just notions of the divine character and glory, to consider such parts of God's procedure as belonging to that *human* mode of representing his mind and will which is adopted throughout Scripture, and adopted from the absolute impossibility of conveying to us otherwise clear and adequate ideas of God. He who is simply spirit, and a spirit in all the essential attributes of being, free from the bounds and limits of a creature—infinite, eternal, unchangeable—can only be made known to us through his image *man*, and *must* be represented as thinking and acting in a human manner. In no other way is it possible for us to obtain a realizing sense of his existence, and so to apprehend his manifestations in providence, as to have our affections interested and our wills determined. "Without these anthropomorphisms," or corporeal and human representations of God, to use the words of Hengstenberg, "we never can speak *positively* of God. He who would disentangle himself from them, as the Deists attempt to do, entirely loses sight of God; while seeking to purify and sublimate the representation of him in the highest possible degree, he is carried, through the illusion of excessive respect, out of all respect. In his anxiety to get rid of human forms, he sinks into nonentities. His relation to God becomes of all others the most untrue, the most unworthy; the nearest is practically to him the farthest, the absolute and essential Being changes for him into a shadow."* And in regard to the expressions in Gen. vi. 6, in which God is declared to have repented that he had made man upon the earth —the strongest, perhaps, in all scripture of the class to which the passage before us belongs—the same author further remarks: " Respect is not had here to the circumstance that God is still glorified *upon* men, though not *in* them, but merely to the destination of man to glorify God with a free and willing mind. Were this man's only, as it certainly is his original destination, God must have repented that he had made the degenerate race of mankind. What God would have done had this one point only come into consideration, he is here represented as having actually done, in order to impress upon the hearts of men how great their corruption was, and how deep was God's abhorrence of their sin."†

In like manner, that God should have issued a proclamation dooming Nineveh to destruction, and, in consideration of the people's repentance, should have recalled the sentence, and repented of the evil he had said he would do to it, this was evidently

* *Authentie,* ii. p. 448.   † Do., p. 453.

with the design of begetting right impressions concerning God's views of sin upon the one hand, and of sincere repentance on the other. Such is his holy indignation against sin, that nothing less than overwhelming and immediate destruction is to be regarded as due to transgressors. And yet, severe as this is, such also is his compassion for the perishing, such his yearning desire to save them from destruction, if he only can do it in consistence with his holiness, that whenever he sees them turning in earnest from their sinful ways, and seeking to him for pardon and acceptance, he cancels the doom, and receives them again to blessing. But this, so far from bespeaking God capricious in his ways, and changeable in the principles of his government, rather manifests him to be, in what alone is of essential moment, unalterably the same. Conducting his administration in righteousness, he *must* change his procedure toward men when their relation toward him becomes changed; as Abraham already perceived when he said, " That be far from thee to slay the righteous with the wicked, and that the righteous should be as the wicked ; shall not the Judge of all the earth do right?" Hence also the word of Ezekiel on this precise point to the captious complainers of his day, who thought that the procedure of God should be the same, whatever might be the conduct of the people : " Hear now, O Israel ! Is not my way equal ? are not your ways unequal ? When a righteous man turneth away from his righteousness, and committeth iniquities and dieth in them; for his iniquity that he hath done shall he die. Again, when the wicked man turneth away from his wickedness that he hath committed, and doeth that which is lawful and right, he shall save his soul alive." And so, when Nineveh had passed from being a theatre of wickedness into a place where God's name was feared and his authority obeyed, the measures of his government fitly partook of a corresponding change; and to have dealt with repenting, as he purposed to have done with corrupt and profligate Nineveh, would have betokened an indifference to the essential distinctions between right and wrong —would have betrayed a disposition to deal with the righteous as with the wicked.

It is simply in regard to these eternal principles of righteousness, that the declarations in scripture are made, which affirm the impossibility of change in God: Such, for example, as the word of Balaam, "God is not a man that he should lie, neither the son of man, that he should repent; hath he said, and shall he not do it? or hath he spoken, and shall he not make it good?" Or the corresponding word of Samuel, which, indeed, is but a re-assertion and new application of the same: "The strength of Israel will not repent; for he is not a man that he should repent." Testimonies of this description have respect to those declarations of God which are so inseparably connected with his inherent and immutable righteousness, as to admit of no room for change in regard even to his external administration. Such was the determination of God to bless Israel in the time of Balaam, and in the manner represented by him; for Israel not only possessed the covenant of God, but stood then within the bonds of the covenant; and the faithfulness of God secured them from harm against the power of any adversary or the enchantment of any diviner—although, when they fell away from the obligations of the covenant, as thousands of them did presently after, and in later times the great mass of the people, the course of the divine procedure *was* changed—the curse, and not the blessing, became their portion. Such, again, was the purpose of God to rend the kingdom from Saul in the time of Samuel; for that proud monarch had departed from the condition on which alone God could permit a king to reign in his stead over the chosen people; he wanted the heart which God indispensably required, and so the determination to remove him, which was but the expression of God's righteous will, was irrevocably fixed. But such representations of God's character argue nothing against the possibility, or even the moral necessity, of a change of administration in a case like that of Nineveh, where, the spiritual relations of the people having become entirely altered, the procedure originally indicated by God of necessity fell to the ground; it could no longer have been enforced in accordance with the essential principles of the government of One who ever delights to manifest himself as at once "a just God and a Saviour."

But this being the case, why, some may be disposed to ask, should the announcement through Jonah have been made to take so absolute a form? Why declare so expressly, that in forty days Nineveh should be destroyed, and not rather, that if the people repented not, such a calamity would certainly overtake them? But what if God knew, as doubtless he did know, that the shape actually given to the message was the best fitted, perhaps the *only* one fitted to awaken the feelings suited to the occasion, and effect the desired result? No doubt, if the thing done had involved any breach of righteous principle,—if the throwing of the message into such a form had been a mere stroke of policy, in itself not conformable to the truth of things, then, however adapted to the end in view, it could not have been employed with the approval and sanction of God. But this was by no means the case. As actually delivered, the message was a real utterance of God's mind and purpose toward Nineveh—considered simply as the place where sin had been rearing its head so offensively against heaven; it was, therefore, in its direct and proper aspect a burden from the Lord on account of sin; and as soon as sin was repented of and abandoned, another state of things, not contemplated in the message, came into being—the *cause* of the impending evil was gone—and there was room for the word to take effect which says, "the curse causeless shall not come." In all such cases the principle announced by the prophet Jeremiah, whether expressly mentioned or not, is to be understood as lying at the foundation of the divine procedure and directing it, " At what instant I shall speak concerning a kingdom, to pluck up, and to pull down, and to destroy; if that nation against whom I have pronounced, turn from their evil, I will repent of the evil that I thought to do unto them " (ch. xviii. 7).

In this passage the principle is distinctly and formally brought out which was exemplified in the Lord's dealing with Nineveh; and applied to that portion generally of the prophetic word, which contains denunciations of coming judgment, it plainly instructs us to regard these denunciations as primarily intimations of God's displeasure on account of sin, and only indirectly and remotely as predictions of events actually to happen in providence. They did not necessarily become events at all; their doing so was a contingency depending on the spiritual condition of the parties respecting whom they were uttered; and to take the burdens of prophecy, as is usually done, in the sense of absolute and determinate judgments that *must* be executed, may lead us in several instances to miss their proper design, and even to place them in opposition to the facts of history. The tide of evil which they poured forth on guilty persons or communities, may have been again checked by a timely reformation from the evil, and what the messenger of God suspended over them simply as a curse, perhaps in process of time passed into a blessing.*

* Look, for example, to the words of Jacob on Simeon an

3. It is clear, however, from the very nature of the principle now under consideration, that it cannot be confined to one side only of the divine administration, but must be equally valid in regard to the other. If a change in man's spiritual relation to him from bad to good necessitates a corresponding change in the manifestations he gives of himself to them, an alteration in the reverse order, from good to bad, must draw along with it a partial, and, if persevered in, a total

Levi, which were the utterance of a comparative curse (only indeed *comparative*, for as children of the covenant they still had a share in the blessing, and hence are said to have been blessed, as well as the rest, by their father): "Cursed be their anger, for it was fierce, and their wrath, for it was cruel ; I will divide them in Jacob, and scatter them in Israel." This sentence on the two brethren, dooming them to future separation and dispersion, was evidently pronounced upon them as a judgment for their past misconduct, and was to take effect on the supposition of the spiritual state of the parents continuing, and even perpetuating itself in their descendants. In the case of Simeon, such appears to have been actually the case ; of all the tribes, it suffered most from God's judgments on the way to Canaan, and entered the land in so enfeebled a condition, that certain cities within the inheritance of the tribe of Judah were appointed for its lot (Joshua xix. 1), whence it appears to have become ulti- mately merged in Judah, and its people are doubtless "the children of Israel that dwelt in the cities of Judah," referred to in 1 Kings xii. 17, as adhering to Rehoboam. (The two tribes forming the kingdom of Judah were thus necessarily Simeon and Judah, with a portion, but only apparently a very small portion, those in and around Jerusalem, of the tribe of Benjamin.—See Hengstenberg on Ps. lxxx. Introd.) Levi, however, from some cause, probably from nothing more than a consideration of the solemn words of the dying patriarch, became pre-eminent among the tribes for piety and zeal ; and though the dispersion threat-

suspension of God's purpose to do them good. And if the *threatenings* of the prophetic word, then of necessity also its *promises*, are not to be regarded as primarily and infallibly predictions of coming events, but rather as exhibitions of the Lord's goodness, free outgoings of his desire, and solemn pledges of his readiness to bless, yet capable of being hindered or restrained by the exercise of a perverse or rebellious spirit on the part of men.

ened might in one sense be said to be carried into effect, yet not properly *as* threatened ; it changed its character when it became the method appointed by God for enabling them to do more efficiently the work of spiritual judges and teachers to their brethren. So far from being necessarily weakened by such a dispersion, it empowered them, so long as they were faithful to their charge, to hold the highest place of influence ; it was only when they proved unfaithful, that their scattering became the source of weakness.

Or, look again, as another example, to the prophecies of Ezekiel respecting Egypt (chap. xxix. xxx.), which declare against it destruction of power, a scattering among the nations, baseness and contempt, and even utter desolation (compare also Joel iii. 19). It is clear, that what the prophet speaks is a denunciation of judgment on account of sin, the sin especially of pride of heart and professing to do for God's people what God alone could perform—and therefore, though the evils threatened did so far alight upon them, yet we have no reason to think that they would be continued beyond the time that the Egyptians were chargeable with the sins in question. There are other prophecies which speak of Egypt as peculiarly the object of divine mercy (in particular, Isaiah xix. 18-25), which *began* to be fulfilled whenever Egypt received the knowledge of God, as it did to a very considerable extent in the first ages of Christianity. And it would be no violation of Ezekiel's word rightly understood, if Egypt even now were rising to an influential position as a nation.

The word of Jeremiah, which most explicitly an-
nounces the principle, and applies it particularly to
nations, is equally express on this side as on the
other: "And at what instant I shall speak concerning a nation, and concerning a kingdom, to build
and to plant it; if it do evil in my sight, that it obey
not my voice, then I will repent of the good where-
with I said I would benefit them. Now therefore go
to, speak to the men of Judah, and to the inhabitants
of Jerusalem, saying, Thus saith the Lord; Behold, I
frame evil against you, and devise a device against
you: return ye now every one from his evil way, and
make your ways and your doings good."—(ch. xviii.
9–11.) Nor is the prophet Ezekiel less express in
his announcement of the principle, and its application
to individuals: "But when the righteous turneth
away from his righteousness, and committeth iniquity,
and doeth according to all the abominations that the
wicked man doeth, shall he live? All his righteousness that he hath done shall not be mentioned; in
his trespass that he hath trespassed, and in his sin
that he hath sinned, in them shall he die."—(ch. xviii.
24.) In like manner also the apostle Paul, extending
the principle to all the promised manifestations of the
Lord's goodness: "Behold therefore the goodness and
severity of God: on them which fell, severity; but
toward thee, goodness, *if thou continue in his goodness
otherwise thou also shalt be cut off.*"—(Rom. xi. 22.)
That is, the word of promise which certifies us of God's
goodness is to be understood as valid only so long as

the spiritual relation contemplated in it continues; when that ceases, a new and different state of things is introduced, for which the promise was not intended, and to which it cannot justly be applied.

Very striking examples of this also have been given in the course of God's providence, as connected with the history of his ancient people. How express, for instance, was the word brought by Moses to the children of Israel in Egypt, that the Lord had heard their groanings, that he was now come to deliver them, and would bring them into the land promised to their fathers! Yet that word, as we might indeed have inferred from the character of God himself, and as subsequent events showed, went entirely on the supposition that they would hearken and be obedient to the voice of God. This, however, the greater portion of them failed so often and to such an extent to do, that the fulfilment of the word in their experience became morally impossible. The prophecies, in like manner, which were given before respecting their future condition in Canaan, that it would be to them a land flowing with milk and honey, that the people should be there replenished with blessings of the heavens above, and blessings of the earth beneath, that they should dwell alone among the nations, satisfied with the favour of God, and should possess it as an everlasting inheritance—such prophecies as these, which were, in other words, promises of mercy and loving-kindness, could not be more than partially verified, because the people obstinately refused to

maintain the relation of filial reverence and love to
God, which was pre-supposed as the common ground
of all blessing.   And of course, as all promises are
prospective, and partake to some extent of the character of prophecies, what has been now said of the
kind of prophecies referred to, may certainly be extended to the promises of blessing generally scattered
throughout Scripture, and addressed to men at large.
The good offered and secured in the promise must
always be understood in connexion with the principles
of holiness; and the grace which reigns in the experience of Christ's people, as well as in the work of
Christ himself, can only reign *through righteousness*
unto eternal life.

But to speak only of what is more strictly understood by the prophetic word, it is clear from what has
been advanced, that if we would give a sound and
consistent interpretation to its utterances, we must
distinguish between one portion and another, and not
throw the whole into one mass, as if, from having all
proceeded from a prophet's lips, it were all to be brought
under one and the same rule.   There are portions of
it which may justly be regarded as in the strictest
sense absolute, because depending for their fulfilment
on nothing but the faithfulness and power of God
Such, for example, are the visions of Daniel respecting
the successive monarchies of the world; such also
the announcements made respecting the appearance
of Christ in the flesh, the line from which he was a
spring, the place where he was to be born, the work

he was to accomplish, and the nature and progress of his kingdom; such, again, the prediction of an apostasy within the Christian Church, and the purely prophetic delineation of things to come in Daniel's " scripture of truth," and the apocalypse of St John. In regard to these predictions and others of a similar description, we have simply to do with the omniscience of God in foreseeing, his veracity in declaring, and his overruling providence in directing what should come to pass. But when, on the other hand, the word of prophecy takes the shape, as it so often does, of threatenings of judgment, or promises of good things to come, the prophetic element is not the first and the determinate thing, which must at all events develop itself, but rather that which is secondary and dependent. It always takes for granted a certain frame of mind and course of behaviour on the part of those interested in its declarations; and before we inquire whether the things occurring in experience precisely correspond with those previously announced in the prophecy, there is a primary question to be settled, How does the spiritual condition of the persons interested agree with what is implied or expressed in the prophetic word?

That this word, in so far as it utters what directly bears on the wellbeing of men, should thus be bound up, for the measure of fulfilment it is to receive, with their spiritual condition, is no expedient devised to meet a difficulty in interpretation. On the contrary, it rests on a principle which is essentially connected

with the nature of God, and is inwoven, we may say,
as a ground-element in all the manifestations he has
given of himself in Scripture.   *There*, from first to
last, all is predominantly of a spiritual or moral, not
simply of a natural character; and, in nothing more
does the religion of the Bible in its entire course differ
from the religions of the world, than in the place it
assigns to the principles of righteousness, ever putting
these first, and subordinating to them all divine
arrangements and purposes.   The evil and the good
here are no mere nature-processes, but results growing
out of the eternal distinctions, which are rooted in the
character of God, between sin and holiness.   It was
the grand error of the Jews in ancient times to forget
this.   Surrounded on every hand by the foul atmo-
sphere of heathenism, which was just the deification
of nature, they were too prone to feel as if they held
their portion of good on merely natural grounds; they
thought their lineal descent from Abraham alone secured them in what was promised, and thus came
practically to disregard God's threatenings on account
of sin, and to convert his promises into absolute and
unconditional titles to blessing.   For *them* a most
pernicious and fatal mistake in experience, as it must
also be for *us* in interpretation, if we should fall in any
degree into their error!   We want the key to a right
interpretation at once of God's threatenings and of his
promises, unless we see them in the mirror of his own
pure righteousness; and we shall unquestionably misunderstand both him and them, if we suppose that

even when he most severely threatens, he can smite the truly repentant sinner or people, or that he can continue to bless the children of promise when they harden their heart against reproof, however expressly and copiously he may have promised to bless.*

* See a fuller development of the principle of interpretation brought out in this chapter in the Supplementary Remarks.

CHAPTER VIII

From the effect produced on the mind of God by the
repentance of Nineveh toward him, we now pass to
the effect produced on the mind of Jonah by the repentance of God toward Nineveh. This at first sight
appears strange, so strange as to seem almost inexplicable in a man who had passed through such singular
experiences, and had been so peculiarly honoured in
his work. "But it displeased Jonah exceedingly, and
he was very angry (or rather, he was very much
grieved or vexed *). And he prayed unto the Lord,
and said, I pray thee, O Lord, was not this my saying, when I was yet in my country? Therefore I
fled before unto Tarshish: for I knew that thou art a

---

* This is evidently the affection meant to be noted here. The
word in the original properly denotes being hot, usually hot with
anger; but as a person may be hot with grief or vexation as well
as anger, the expression is used also of this. So, for example, of
David in 2 Sam. vi. 8, where David is said to have been *displeased*
(hot) at the breach God had made on Uzzah; the meaning plainly
is that he was distressed and grieved.

gracious God, and merciful, slow to anger, and of great kindness, and repentest thee of the evil. Therefore now, O Lord, take, I beseech thee, my life from me; for it is better for me to die than to live. And the Lord said, Doest thou well to be angry?" The marginal reading here is nearer the proper meaning, but it should be, as the Septuagint correctly renders it, Art thou very much grieved? *

* The rendering of the expression here, and in the other verses where it occurs, given in the authorized version, Doest thou well to be angry? has been an unhappy error, as it has tended greatly to countenance and keep up the mistaken view that has prevailed regarding Jonah's character. As the words stand in the original, they form a sort of phrase, or idiomatic turn of expression, and every one knows, that what seems to be a literal translation of such modes of speech, will often be very far from a correct representation of the meaning. For example, the expression, "He is at great pains to improve his mind," would perhaps be very naturally turned by a German or an Italian into words which signified, that the person meant put himself to severe agony to secure his improvement; yet a less literal rendering would give a much correcter idea of the meaning. So here. The Greek translator of the Septuagint, by much the oldest version of Old Testament Scripture, perfectly understood the expression, and expressed it well by words answering to those given above, Art thou very much grieved? The Syriac expresses the same meaning, and so also the learned Jew, Kimchi, who adds, "As for היטב, it imports the strengthening of a subject;" i. e., merely denotes here that the grief or vexation was very great. Henderson, in his work on the Minor Prophets, properly renders it, "Art thou much vexed?" though he still fails to take a just estimate of the character and feelings of Jonah. The mistake, so often repeated in the versions, arose from not adverting to the use of the infinite absol. of the Hebrew verb יטב, which is often taken as an adverb, and can then only be rendered by *very much*, *greatly*, or *exceedingly*. See the Lexicons.

Why should Jonah have been so displeased and vexed, and rendered even weary of life, by an event which one would think fitted to inspire thankfulness and joy into every well-constituted mind? " Because," says Calvin, expressing the general view of commentators, " he was unwilling to appear as a vain and lying prophet." And Dr Adam Clarke, whetting the matter a little more sharply upon poor Jonah, says, " He had more respect to his high sense of his own honour, than he had to the goodness and mercy of God. He appeared to care little whether 620,000 persons were destroyed or not, so he might not pass for a deceiver, or one that denounced a falsity." This, indeed, is the view that very naturally suggests itself on a somewhat hasty and superficial consideration of the subject; and yet there is something about the circumstances of Jonah, something even in the very account given of his vexation, which can scarcely fail to beget a conviction of there being a still deeper ground for the painful feelings that agitated his mind. For, if Jonah was so greatly to blame here, if his own credit with the world stood so high in his esteem, that he would rather have seen the largest city on the earth buried in ruins, than that he should be exposed to the taunt from thoughtless and inconsiderate persons (for such alone in the circumstances *could express* it) of having spoken what had not literally taken place, he must have belonged, we shall not say to the lowest class of saints, but to the worst specimens of humanity; he must have had the breast of a demon,

rather than of a man.   And such Dr Clarke not ob-
scurely insinuates was the case, when he asks, " Who
but he who is of a fiendish nature will be grieved
because God's mercy triumphs over judgment?"

But this is plainly to give a darker view of Jonah's
character and conduct than the circumstances of the
case warrant, or than is borne out by the later allusions of scripture respecting him.   Had such been
really the ground of Jonah's uneasiness he would
have deserved the severest rebuke and chastisement,
especially considering what he had already suffered
from warring against the mind and purposes of God.
And yet the Lord does no more than mildly expos-
tulate with him, and, by a course of treatment much
more remarkable for its gentleness and condescension
than for its severity, tries to convince him of his
mistake.   Not only so ; but, when we come down to
New Testament times, we find such honourable mention made of Jonah, and such a close resemblance
drawn by our Lord himself between his own mission
as a prophet and that of Jonah's, that we cannot rest
with satisfaction in the view suggested above.   We
cannot believe such marked and honourable reference
would have been made to him, if he had been the
selfish, perverse, unreasonable creature he is represented to have been ; but are rather driven to the
conviction, that deeper views and less discreditable
feelings gave the tone to his behaviour here, than such
as a hasty glance might naturally dispose one to
imagine.

Besides, viewing the matter even on the lowest ground, and with reference to the prophet's repute in the world, it must surely have appeared to any one but the most depraved or childish being, a far more ennobling distinction to have been, under God, the reformer of a great people and the saviour of their city, than simply to have been known as the herald who had truly announced its doom. Though what he proclaimed had not literally taken place, his preaching was still the instrumental cause of saving the city from ruin; and if carnal ambition had wrought in his bosom—if worldly honour, in reality, was the jewel so dear to him—it seems hard to understand why he should have wished an opposite result, at least so passionately wished it as to have longed for death because he had been disappointed in the object of his desire.

But what reason have we to suppose that Jonah's vexation and concern turned at all upon the point of his own veracity, and, as connected with that, his reputation in the world? This is nowhere expressed, nor even hinted at in the text, and is but an inference hastily and unwarrantably drawn, from there being apparently no other motive at hand to account for such keen dissatisfaction and pungent sorrow in the prophet's bosom. It is carefully to be noted, however, that in his address to God not only is no stress laid upon the failure of the prediction, but no mention whatever is made of it; the exercise of the divine clemency, and the saving of Nineveh from destruction, is the whole that is brought into view. So much had the thought of this weighed upon the prophet's feelings, weighed even as a depressing load upon the energies of his mind, that he alleges it now as the main reason why he had at first shunned the charge committed to him, and fled to Tarshish. But the charge then given, it will be remembered, did not require Jonah to announce the destruction of Nineveh; it simply required him to cry against the Ninevites, because their sins were crying for vengeance in the ear of God. This would certainly have betokened that they were in danger of the divine judgments; but it would not have placed Jonah in a position in which he run any risk of having his veracity impeached. It was only on the second commission being given that the word put into his mouth took the definite form of a proclamation, that the city should be overthrown in forty days. Yet, in the expression he now gave to his feelings, he appears to have entirely overleapt this new turn of affairs, and throws himself back upon the original ground of dissatisfaction—he is vexed and chagrined for no other reason, so far as we can judge, than that there was here a new exercise of the divine forbearance, and a city spared that had deserved to go to perdition. This precisely is the point we have to account for: Why should such a manifestation of the divine goodness have sunk so heavily upon the soul of this man of God? why, when apparently gaining, beyond all reasonable expectation, the great end for which he

had come to exercise in Nineveh the calling of a prophet, should he have regarded the very success of his
mission as taking from him all that was worth living
for?

It is manifest, from the simple stating of the question, that Jonah must have viewed his mission to
Nineveh, not as an ultimate thing, but as occupying
the relation of means to an end—as connected with
some other object of pre-eminent importance, to which
he thought it should have been made altogether subservient. If Nineveh alone had been concerned, he
could not but have rejoiced in the result actually obtained; but there was an ulterior and higher object
in his eye, on which it seemed to tell so unfavourably,
that sorrow the most pungent filled his heart. And
to learn what this object was, we have no need to
travel into the regions of conjecture; we have only
to think of his calling as a prophet in Israel, and to
suppose him bent on the attainment of its great end,
the spiritual and temporal good of the people—like
every true prophet, finding in that the thing for which
he lived and breathed. This we are not only warranted, but bound, to regard as the paramount consideration in Jonah's mind; and he must somehow
have come to regard the destruction of Nineveh as
fitted to act most powerfully in promoting it, and the
preservation of Nineveh most disastrously in hinder-
ing it. How should he have thought thus?

We must bear in mind, while we inquire into the
matter, that the book which contains the record of

Jonah's relation to Nineveh, possesses for the Church somewhat of the nature of a parable; what it reports is to be regarded as an acted lesson—an instruction from God under the cover of a history. Like every thing of this description, it has a deeper meaning than meets the eye at first; it requires to be thought upon and pondered by the people of God, otherwise they are sure to fail in catching its true design, and to miss the important truths with which it is fraught. This is evident from the use our Lord makes of it, gathering, as he does, from this history of Jonah and his work at Nineveh, a voice that reached even to the men of his own generation, and discovering in it a sign which called for their especial notice and regard. How much more must the things it records, when known as current transactions, have been a sign to the generation itself in Israel, among whom the prophet lived and laboured! And how much did it concern them to listen to the voice which spake through these events for their instruction and warning, and to make themselves acquainted with its fullest import!

The people of that generation, as we before saw, were in the last stages of degeneracy, and trembling on the brink of ruin. All efforts had hitherto failed to recover them from idolatry and corruption; and the Lord, before finally abandoning them to their fate, sought once more to move them from their course, by working upon them through feelings of jealousy and shame. For this purpose he stept out of the usual tenor of his way, and did the marvellous work in Nineveh we have already discoursed of—exhibiting there the example of a people, who repented at the preaching merely of one prophet and on the deliverance of one message—and were thereby saved from impending ruin. What God really meant to teach the people of Israel by this example, was the inexcusable character of their own impenitence if they should still continue to persevere in it, and the inevitable certainty of the destruction which in that case must alight upon them. Repenting Nineveh had proved herself more deserving of the divine favour than backsliding and apostate Israel; the children of the covenant had not only sunk to a level with the heathen, but in comparison of this particular people had fallen visibly below them: therefore the outward relations also must be changed—Israel go down, the heathen rise to distinction.

Now, it is surely not unreasonable to suppose, that when Jonah saw how bent the Lord was on sending him to Nineveh, and what a wonder had been wrought in his own experience to have a work of God accomplished there, he might have come to understand that the work was intended to have an important bearing on the kingdom of Israel; while yet it is more than probable, from having his eye intent only upon one great point, that he might misapprehend the precise kind of bearing which the Lord chiefly intended it to have. Living in the days of the second Jeroboam, when a new tide of prosperity had been constantly flowing in upon the kingdom of Israel, and had given rise to an almost universal dissoluteness and profligacy, he had the mortification, not only to labour long comparatively in vain, but also to witness a growing declension among the people, who thought they could afford, amid the fulness of their sufficiency, to slight his admonitions and despise his warnings. In such painful circumstances, how could he avoid sighing for some remarkable suspension of the forbearance and goodness of God, which they were so shamefully abusing? some salutary visitation of judgment which might startle them from their false security, and convince them effectually that destruction was certain to overtake the transgressors? Oh! where—we can conceive him to have exclaimed—where is the Lord God of Elijah? Where is the arm of might that in his days caused its thunders to be heard by the deadest heart, and with terrible things in righteousness arrested the people when they were rushing onward to the gulf of ruin? The awful retributions of justice which were then inflicted, are too long past to be remembered now; overflowing prosperity has filled the hearts of the people with madness; and if the Lord does not speedily avenge his cause by some new displays of severity, all will soon be irretrievably lost.

Thus we can easily understand how Jonah might feel discouraged and oppressed most of all by the thought of the Lord's clemency and goodness—how this might even hang as a deadening load upon his mind, when the commission was first given him to go to Nineveh, leading him to regard the work of reform assigned to him there as a hopeless undertaking; and how he might despair of any thing effectual being done in the cause of God, unless there were first given a striking example of severity. We can also easily understand how readily he would imagine, when he actually stood within the precincts of Nineveh, and had received the command to proclaim its downfal in forty days, that now at last he was to obtain that very example of severity which he had conceived to be so needful—that the Lord was indeed going to vindicate the honour of his name upon wicked transgressors, by making even proud Nineveh, like Sodom and Gomorrah, a monument of ruin—and that, from witnessing this awful display of judgment, he would go back to resume his labours among his own people, with such an argument as he never had before, and could never expect to have again, to persuade their return from sin to the love and service of God.

Such then, being, as we have every reason to believe, the state of Jonah's mind, it requires no stretch of imagination to conceive what a grievous disappointment it would be for him to see Nineveh still spared, and the very weapon wrested out of his hand by which he had hoped to prevail with his thoughtless and rebellious countrymen. It was not that he was a man of a proud humour, or a merciless disposition, and could have looked with fiendish delight on the overthrow of that great city; but that he loved his own people so intensely, and was so firmly persuaded that an act of severity was required to arouse them from their false security—it was this, which caused his bosom to burn with vexation when he found Nineveh was still to be spared. For how could he return again to speak to his degenerate countrymen? What hope could he any longer have of labouring with success among them? How certainly would they look to the outward result merely of the case, and take new courage to go on in their sins by this new manifestation of the mercy and forbearance of God? Instead of having reached a higher vantage-ground, from which to urge their return to God, he felt as if a signal discouragement had been thrown in his way; and it seemed now, that nothing more remained for him to say or to do—it were even better for him to die than to live.

Jonah's state of mind on this occasion appears to have been very similar to that of Elijah, at the memorable period when he fled from the face of Jezebel into the wilderness. After long waiting for some decisive turning-point in the grand controversy that was then proceeding between Jehovah and Baal, he had at last found what he sought; in the presence of all Israel the fire of heaven had come down and consumed the Lord's sacrifice on Carmel, so that the hearts of the people seemed to be at once turned back again to Jehovah, and with one consent they rose up and slew the prophets of Baal. In the exultation of the moment Elijah thought the conflict was now ended; Jehovah had given the most striking display of his presence and glory that could reasonably be expected, and apparently with triumphant success. But when he heard that the immediate effect on Jezebel was only to rouse her enmity into greater fury, and that she had vowed to be revenged on him by the shedding of his blood, the disappointment was too great even for that iron-nerved prophet to bear with equanimity; and in the recoil of feeling which arose from seeing such hopes and efforts vanishing in fruitlessness, he besought the Lord to take away his life. He had spent his last arrow, and it proved unsuccessful—why should he live any longer on the earth? Such precisely seems to have been Jonah's feeling. After long labouring in vain, and enduring much faintness of spirit on account of the prevailing heedlessness and profligacy, he had been brought to the very verge of an event which promised, if it had occurred, to operate with mighty power upon the hearts of the people, and bring, as it were, a new element of life into the corrupting mass—and all suddenly failed! he found himself again where he was, and with prospects even worse than before; so that life was no longer desirable.

In the case of neither of these prophets was this state of feeling right. It was the offspring of infirmity, such as naturally arose from partial views of the purposes of God, and hasty judgments respecting his procedure; but still it was the infirmity of noble minds—minds consumed with zeal for the glory of God and the spiritual good of men, and feeling as if life for them had ceased to be a boon, when the high ends for which they mainly held it appeared to be no longer attainable. Such a state of feeling is indeed too lofty, it moves in too elevated a region of spiritual being, to be properly sympathized with by the common run even of religious persons. But *they* can sympathize with it who have known what it is to have had their hearts set upon the doing of some great work for the welfare of their fellow-men, and have seen a cloud of chilling disappointment coming between them and the object of their beneficent labours. Especially can *they* sympathize with it who have dedicated themselves with their whole heart to the work of the ministry, and have known in their own experience the crushing effect of labours defeated of their design, and hopes most fondly cherished becoming for ever shipwrecked—*they* can understand how the men of God, who, against fearful odds and in evil times, had to maintain the cause of righteousness, might experience, when the conflict went sore against them, such a sinking of soul as would lead them to prefer death rather than life; and God himself, who knows our frame, can also understand and sympathize with it. Hence his method of dealing with the infirmity in the instances referred to, is so remarkable for its tenderness and condescension; while we see him throwing no cloak over it, on the one hand, we hear him bringing against it no severe reproach or heavy condemnation

on the other; he graciously stoops to press the fainting spirit to his bosom, and, like an affectionate
parent, plies it with such gentle and timely correc-
tives as are fitted to restore it to healthfulness and
vigour.

It is well, indeed, for persons of a soft and easy
sentimentalism to denounce such moods of soul in
heaven's nobler witnesses for the truth, as wild outbursts of passion or the workings of a gloomy fanati-
cism; and to reserve their sympathy for those who
can coolly wait upon the tides of mercy, and, with
evil only appearing, can still please themselves with
the hope that all may come right at the last. Theirs
is a cheap philanthropy. They know nothing of that
vicarious benevolence which identifies itself with the
objects of its regard, and makes their interests and
dangers its own. But wherever the spirit of this
higher benevolence breathes, men feel that they have
to do with stern realities when handling the burden
of sin and the woes of retribution; there is a death-
like earnestness and severity in their struggle with
evil; their very life and happiness is bound up with
the issue. Hence, so long as the hope of success ani-
mates their bosom, there is nothing in labour or suffering they will not readily undergo; and if, when
that hope fails them, their hand should forget its
skill to work, their heart become faint, life itself cease
to be desirable, they but prove themselves to be still
compassed about with human infirmity; they have
not reached the matchless virtue which no discourage-

ment can overpower. But never surely can men be
fitter objects of tenderness and pity than when thus
broken and oppressed in spirit; and never can railing
accusation be more grievously misplaced than when
directed against them in such a time of nature's weakness and misgiving.

Let us learn, however, even from the failures of
such giant warriors in the service of God. Elijah
and Jonah both erred from taking too limited and
partial a view of God's power and purposes, though
by looking in somewhat different directions. Elijah
had seen a display of God's severity; but was disappointed and grieved because the spiritual result had
not sprung from it so immediately and to such an extent as he had expected. He did not yet know,
though he came in process of time to learn, how deep
a work of reformation had already commenced, and
how much he might still be enabled to do to help it
forward, not so much by weapons of terror, as by the
" still small voice" of counsel, admonition, and encouragement, uttered from house to house among the
thousands of Israel. Jonah again erred, because,
not being permitted to see a display of severity, he
thought the only measure was withheld which could
effectually promote the interests of godliness, and
nothing remained for him but to witness anew, and
on a still larger scale than before, the wanton abuse
of God's mercy and forbearance. He did not yet
know that the Lord had important purposes to serve
by this example of mercy to the penitent, such as could

not have been accomplished by an example of severity
on the unbelieving and profligate. He did not know
this; but he should in faith and patience have waited
for the development of God's purposes, believing that
there *were* important purposes to be developed, only
lying beyond the ken of his present apprehension.
Indeed, he was too outward in his view—he looked
too little to the *repentance* of Nineveh—perhaps
was at too little pains to make himself acquainted
with its earnest and extensive character—fixed his
eye too exclusively on the mere external movements
of providence; and with his soul bent only on one
great end, took no thought how the result actually
obtained might be made to tell on other ends still
more important, and how it might serve beyond
any other plan to display the manifold wisdom of
God. Could Jonah have foreseen the place those
transactions at Nineveh were to hold in the history of
the world, and the use to be made of them by the in-
carnate Word himself, how readily would he have acquiesced in what was actually done! How cheerfully
would he have exclaimed, "He hath done all things
well; he is wonderful in counsel, and excellent in
working!"

The lesson for us, then, is, that God's way is still
the best; for he sees the end from the beginning, and
directs all with infinite skill and unerring wisdom.
If we *could* alter in any particular the plan of Providence, it would not be for the better, but for the worse.
And though there are trials at times meeting us in the

path of duty, for the present painful to be borne, yet it is at once our duty and our wisdom to take all patiently. In due time we shall reap, if we faint not; and as God's will *must* prevail, there is no burden which impatience will not aggravate, no labour or affliction which, through patience, may not become a blessing.

CHAPTER IX

GOD'S WAYS VINDICATED, AND THE PROPHET'S VIEWS
RECTIFIED AND ENLARGED.

IT would seem, from the concluding portion of the
narrative, that the Divine purpose respecting Nineveh
had been communicated somewhat gradually to Jonah,
and that he had not been at the first certified of the
absolute recall of the threatened judgment. A present suspension of the judgment appears to have been
all that meanwhile became known to him ; and the
apprehension still lingered in his bosom, that some
display of severity would take place, only at a later
period, or in a less appalling form than had been
announced. He could not yet believe that matters
would be allowed to resume their former course of
peace and prosperity, without a strong demonstration
given from above of the guilt of former iniquities.
And in this belief—not from any sullenness of temper, as is often gratuitously imagined, but merely
with the design of observing, as from a watch-tower,
the march of Divine providence, yet imperfectly disclosed to him—" he went out of the city, and sat

on the east side of the city, and there made him a
booth, and sat under it in the shadow, till he might
see what would become of the city."

The brief account of this part of the transactions
renders it impossible for us to speak with certainty
of the ground of Jonah's views and expectations.
We cannot suppose that he was so utterly ignorant
of the repentance that had taken place among the
people, or so little acquainted with the principles of
the Divine government, as to have looked for precisely the same kind and measure of severity now,
that would have been suitable if no decided effect
had been produced by his preaching. Neither of
these suppositions can be regarded as in the least
degree credible. But there is no improbability in
supposing, that, both from his position as a stranger,
and from the peculiar character of the mission given
him to discharge in Nineveh, Jonah was but imperfectly acquainted with the spirit of repentance awakened among its people; nor is it unlikely that he
was aware of many who had not undergone any real
change—*so many* as might warrant, in his own mind,
the belief that judgment, to some extent, might still
righteously be executed. And there is also room for
entertaining another thought respecting him. With
all that he felt and spake of the richness of God's
mercy and goodness, he might, even with a conviction of the general penitence of the people, have
judged a certain degree of severity perfectly compatible with God's righteousness. This, it must be

remembered, was a point on which the economy of
the Old Testament shed a comparatively defective
light.   There is nowhere in that portion of God's
revelations which had been given before the time of
Jonah, such a manifestation of sovereign grace, freely
and at once restoring the penitent sinner to the full
enjoyment of God's favour and blessing, as can once
be compared to that unfolded in the parable of the
prodigal son.   The dispensation of Moses peculiarly
failed here, being adapted throughout—and, from its
shadowy and imperfect nature, necessarily adapted—
to impress more upon men's convictions the evil and
condemnation of sin, than to lay open to them the
riches of Divine beneficence.   Accordingly, David's
repentance, though betokening the most intense sorrow and remorse on account of sin, did not save him
from certain painful executions of judgment.   And
Jonah's own experience also, driven forth, as he had
been, like a forlorn outcast into the deep, after the
most pungent feelings of contrition had been awakened
in his bosom, had only brought a new proof of the
judgment which was then wont to mingle so much
with mercy in the procedure of God.   Can we, then,
be surprised if he should have deemed it probable
that Nineveh, even when repenting, might be visited
with tokens of displeasure, though the doom originally
threatened was no longer to be enforced?   We must
endeavour to picture his state of mind, not from a
New, but from an Old Testament point of view; and
remember that, though he was a prophet, he still had

to take his ideas of God's character and dealings from the comparatively imperfect pattern of things belonging to the dispensation under which he lived.

These considerations appear to me perfectly sufficient to account for a state of mind in Jonah such as might induce him, without any disobedience to the will of God, so far as that had yet been made known to him, to go and erect a booth at some distance from the city, where he might wait in anxious expectation to see what would become of it. What he still needed to learn, and what he must also be taught to acquiesce in, was the largeness of the mercy to be extended to Nineveh—that it amounted to an entire remission of the threatened penalty. And, partly to convey to him this instruction, partly also to commend it to him as reasonable and just, nay, as of essential moment to the best interests of the Divine kingdom, his temporary lodging was turned for him into a school of discipline, and he was taught, from the things of his own experience, to rise to higher and more enlightened views of the procedure of God. In transcribing the account of this transaction, we must take leave to substitute the Septuagint rendering, for that in the common version, of the peculiar phrase explained in a note at the beginning of last chapter, and simply notice, by way of information to those who may need it, that what are called booths in Scripture are temporary frames or sheds, hastily run up with slender bits of wood, and presenting many openings, through which either wind or heat may penetrate. "And the Lord God prepared a gourd,* and made it to come up over Jonah, that it might be a shadow over his head, to deliver him from his grief. [Mark here the proof incidentally given of the real affection under which Jonah laboured— *grief*, not anger.] So Jonah was exceeding glad of the gourd. But God prepared a worm when the morning rose the next day, and it smote the gourd that it withered. And it came to pass, when the sun beat upon the head of Jonah, that he fainted, and wished in himself to die, and said, It is better for me to die than to live. And God said to Jonah, Art thou very much grieved for the gourd? And he said, I am very much grieved, even to death. Then said the Lord, Thou hast had pity on the gourd, for the which thou hast not laboured, neither madest it grow, which came up in a night, and perished in a night: and should I not spare Nineveh, that great city, wherein are more than sixscore thousand persons that cannot discern between their right hand and their left hand; and also much cattle?"

While undergoing this salutary and instructive pro-

---

* It is of no moment, as to the meaning of the passage, what the particular plant might be which is here denominated *gourd*, or whether this may be its proper designation. The Hebrew name is *kikajon*, and seems to be the same with the Egyptian *kiki*, the common *ricinus*, or castor-oil plant, sometimes also called *palm-crist*, the name adopted in the margin of our Bibles. This plant is known to be very common in the East, and, from its broad foliage and the softness of its stem, answers well to the description of the text.

cess, Jonah appears at different stages in two very different, and even opposite, frames of mind. But in both alike it has fared with him according to the proverb, "We have piped to you, and ye have not danced; we have mourned, and ye have not wept." For in the one he has been represented as a poor sensual creature, "rejoicing in his creature-comforts," and thinking all was well if he could but enjoy himself a little under the refreshing shade of his temporary gourd; while in the other he is charged with giving way to pettish and malignant humours, having "a bosom that swelled with anger," and continuing still self-willed, and "so intractable as even to contend with God." So the author of Jonah's portraiture;* and another, but much older, delineator, handles him a little more roughly still: "Was there ever man under heaven so testy and peevish, to chop thus with his Maker, and still the further he goeth, the more to be out of square?" The author denounces "the rigour of his fury and the cruelty of his stomach," and holds him up to reprobation as one "so filled with choler that he fretted and chafed with the Lord."† Matters have not grown better for Jonah as the world has grown older; for a more recent delineator than either of the preceding, the late venerable author of a practical exposition of the book of Jonah, represents the prophet as exhibiting at this time "a

* The Rev. Thomas Jones.

† Abbot's Exposition upon the Prophet Jonah, vol. ii. lect. xxvii. xxviii.

proud, sullen, and discontented spirit"—as a person of such rare and desperate malignity, that "he could turn the very goodness of God into a ground of accusation against him"—as presenting a sight so odious that imagination cannot picture to itself one more revolting— and needlessly plunging himself into distress from the violence of his own unhallowed temper.* But if the case were so with Jonah, we surely must, in consistence, forego his claim to be considered even yet a subject of grace; for he must then be regarded as going off the stage in a most presumptuous opposition to God—not only rebelling against the Divine will, but also "defending his rebellious conduct." And if the man of whom this could be said in truth—and said, too, at the close of a most remarkable train of providences, fitted, if any thing could be, to cure a perverse spirit of its waywardness—if that man was still a child of God, there must have been a peculiarity in his case, for which we shall look in vain for any parallel in Scripture; and the worst symptoms of nature's depravity must be held quite compatible with the existence of the life of God.

By much the greater portion of these hard charges against Jonah arise from the mistaken view entertained of his character, as being a man chiefly concerned about his own reputation, coupled with the false translation, which not only ascribes to him the passion of anger, instead of grief, but also gives him the appearance of justifying himself in his anger.

* Dr Peddie's Lectures on Jonah, ix. and x.

Having already removed these grounds of misappre-
hension, we have the less difficulty in viewing the
behaviour of Jonah on the present occasion in a more
favourable light, and also in discerning some higher
reasons for the treatment of God toward him, than if
it aimed merely at the dislodgement of a foolish and
fretful humour from his bosom. Jonah was discon-
certed and downcast because the example of severity
had been withheld, which he thought would operate
so beneficially upon the minds of his countrymen, and
without which he seemed to have no means of attain-
ing the great end and object of his life. What, in
such circumstances, was needed to rectify his mistake
and restore him to a better mind? It was plainly
something that would turn his thoughts out of that
one channel in which they were so determinately
running, and presenting to him other ends to be accomplished by the transactions at Nineveh than had
yet entered his imagination to conceive.

For this purpose the Lord permitted him to go and
construct his frail booth in the neighbourhood of the
city, and to experience there for a time great uneasiness from the glowing heat of a vertical sun and a
parching wind. He then suddenly brought over him
the shadow of a broad foliage, by the extraordinary
growth of a little plant, but this only to make him
feel more intensely the force of the noxious elements
to which he was exposed, by again as suddenly causing the plant to wither, so that Jonah fainted under
the distress that came upon him, and would have

found death itself a happy release. The instrument
through which this overpowering effect was produced
may seem very small in itself, and scarcely adequate
to the occasion; but it must be viewed in connexion
with the attendant circumstances, and especially with
the mental depression under which Jonah laboured.
It was, besides, precisely such a thing as was fitted to
shut his mouth in regard to God's dealing with Nineveh; and not only to do that, but, at the same time,
to let in a flood of light upon his soul respecting the
purposes which that dealing was destined to advance.
For what room was left for dissatisfaction or complaint when the Lord proceeded to ask him how—
since he would so willingly have spared this little
gourd, and grieved so much for its loss because its presence had been refreshing to him—he could not much
rather justify God in sparing the large city of Nineveh, the dwelling-place of such myriads of living beings, and the subject of so much paternal anxiety and
care? Must there not be some unhappy bias in the
mind which so keenly felt the destruction of the one,
and so ardently longed for the destruction of the
other?

Yes; but perhaps it may be thought that this
scarcely meets the point mainly at issue. For the
matter seems here to be put simply on natural grounds;
the appeal is only made from the comparative insig-
nificance of the plant to the gigantic magnitude of
the city, and the little concern Jonah had with the
one·to the great concern God had with the other; and

in these respects there was no room even for a moment's hesitation as to the answer that should be returned to the question addressed to the prophet. But might not Jonah still have rejoined, or at least silently reflected in his mind, that it was not on natural, but on spiritual, grounds he had sought the execution of judgment on Nineveh—that he had desired this merely on account of the vindication it was fitted to give of God's righteousness, and its tendency to promote the advancement of his kingdom in Israel; while the sparing of the gourd or the city, considered in respect to the littleness of the one and the magnitude and importance of the other, was a thing confined only to the region of nature? No doubt, he might have so rejoined if he had looked to the mere surface of the transaction; but viewing what was said and done—as he could not avoid doing—in the light of a parable, concealing under the outward veil a deep moral import, he would soon discover the entire suitableness of the instruction to the matter in hand. The natural, which is alone in both cases distinctly brought into view, was but a ladder through which the mind of the prophet might rise to corresponding spiritual reflections; and the key to the spiritual lies in the *need* which Jonah for the time had of the foliage of the gourd. In other circumstances it might have been a matter of entire indifference to him what happened to the plant, whether it had been spared or destroyed; but, situated as he then was, depending for his comfort, and in a sense also for his life, on its ample foliage, its sudden destruction necessarily came upon him as a sore calamity. And such now the Lord would have him to consider was the case in respect to Nineveh, as a city that feared the name and obeyed the voice of the Lord: in the sad degeneracy of the times, God's cause had need of it, and would suffer damage by its overthrow, much as Jonah's material wellbeing had suffered by the withering of the gourd.

If Israel had been faithful to his calling, and had fulfilled aright his original destination, to be himself holiness to the Lord, and a light amidst the surrounding heathenism, then, indeed, the Lord might have dispensed with any special service from Nineveh. Or, if there had been any hope of the people in the kingdom of Israel being still brought permanently to a better mind by some great example of severity falling out in their neighbourhood, he might have been less intent on the repentance and preservation of Nineveh. But this hope could no longer be entertained. Every thing had already been tried with them of that description which was likely to tell with effect on their spiritual condition. Judgments of the most appalling kind had time after time been wrought among themselves, and had once and again reduced them to the brink of absolute and utter ruin, yet never with any thing more than a very partial and transient effect: as soon as prosperity again returned, the evil broke forth anew as foully and flagrantly as before. It was by other means than even the most stunning judgment on such a city as Nineveh that God must now work, if any important result was to be achieved among the profligate subjects of Jeroboam; he must call their jealousy into exercise; and by the example of a great people suddenly reformed and spared as a token of Divine favour and blessing, arouse them, if possible, to the alarming consideration, that the kingdom of heaven was ready to retire from its ancient seat, and be transplanted to another which would more willingly yield its spiritual fruits. Yes, the Lord at this time peculiarly had *need* of Nineveh in its now reformed condition; the cause of righteousness in the earth could ill afford to spare so singular a witness to the truth; the spiritual good of Israel itself in particular required it ; and the tidings which the prophet could now carry back of Nineveh's repentance and happy rescue from impending destruction, would be found, if properly understood and believed, far more fitted than the news of its overthrow could have been, to operate with power upon the hearts of his countrymen, and recall them to the true worship and service of God.

This was the course of procedure specially adapted to the condition of backsliding Israel; and yet the Lord knew well beforehand, that even this would fail to produce any general and permanent effect upon their minds. He knew that the time must speedily arrive when the seed of Jacob—those of Ephraim first, and then those of Judah—should be cast out of the inheritance, and scattered among the nations. And though the event would necessarily fall as a terrible disaster upon the people at large, yet for the small remnant who feared the Lord, or such as might then be inclined to turn to him, it was not by any means to prove an unmitigated evil; there would be hope for them even in what might seem to the eye of sense to be their latter end; and in the background of this dealing of God with Nineveh there lay a promise of good for the period of exile itself. The thought that, however the things which had happened in Nineveh might tell upon Israel, they must first be viewed in respect to its own people; that in this primary point of view they possessed an inherent importance, and were fitted to conduce most materially to the glory of God—this thought, which the Lord plainly sought from the first to impress upon Jonah, and which was embodied anew in the matter-of-fact parable of the gourd, provided for all the faithful among the coming exiles a sure ground of consolation and hope. They were thus taught beforehand, by a most illustrious example, that something might be done for God beyond the bounds of the land of Canaan, which might greatly tend to spread the knowledge of his name and advance the interests of his kingdom. They had failed, as a people, *in* Canaan to fulfil their destiny to be witnesses for the truth of God in the world, and a blessing to the nations of the earth; but this destiny, they would now see, might still in great part be accomplished even when they were banished *from* Canaan and scattered among the nations; the work of Jonah at Nineveh might on a small scale be perpetually repeating itself. And this reflection would lie the nearer to them, as Jonah himself, before he was so highly honoured of God in Nineveh, had also undergone the treatment of an outcast and borne the punishment of his sin; his history stood before them as a palpable proof, that their outcast condition would prove no obstruction to their future usefulness in the service of God. If they would but faithfully apply themselves to what God required at their hands, he would, notwithstanding the evils that befell them, give effect to their testimony and render them a blessing. So that the result of Jonah's mission to Nineveh, while it rung a solemn warning in the ears of the backsliding and wicked in Israel, proclaiming the certainty of their overthrow if they repented not, opened up at the same time for the good a way to honour and enlargement in the things of God, which the darkest events in providence might not prevent them from occupying with honour and success.

Indeed, we cannot but think that this prospective lesson, furnished by the transactions at Nineveh and the parable of the gourd, though not the most immediate and direct, was still a very prominent object in the divine purposes. There are tides in the history of the world, as well as in the private affairs of men; and matters were now approaching a great crisis in that region of the world, which required to be met by a new turn in the outward destination of his Church. How the course of providence might have been ordered in respect to the nations of the earth, if the Israelites had continued a holy and united people, diffusing light and blessing around, it is not for us now to conjecture. But as it had become too clearly manifest that this was no longer to be expected, the Lord permitted a succession of huge monarchies to arise, over which it was in the nature of things impossible for Israel to obtain a political ascendancy, or, while standing apart, to exert any important influence. Yet Israel must still be, as God had promised to Abraham, the appointed channel of blessing to the nations; and the question was, how could this calling now be best fulfilled? Not simply by maintaining their ancient position in Canaan; they must get somehow nearer the helm of affairs, and have the opportunity of reaching the springs of action in the world; and this they could only do by being broken up and scattered, and to some extent intermingled with the nations. Jonah in Nineveh now, Daniel and his holy comrades in Babylon afterwards, were to serve for signs to Israel of the manner in which the people of God were henceforth to display his banner, and influence for his glory the current of events.

Besides, in process of time the great stream of power and dominion among men was to take a new direction, and flow into other channels than it had hitherto done. Long before the era of redemption,

Nineveh and Babylon were to be laid in ruins, and the sceptre which had been wielded by them was to be transferred to entirely different regions of the world. At that era it was not Syria, or the adjacent countries to the north, but Asia Minor, Northern Africa, Greece, Rome, and the southern parts of Europe, which formed the seats of intelligence and power, and from which the influence was to come that should mould the future destinies of the world. Hence, however necessary it may have been for the Jews as a separate people to regain possession of the land of Canaan, and sojourn there till redemption was brought in, it was not less necessary and important, that they should also be found scattered in considerable numbers through the regions referred to, so as to be able to spread abroad the leaven of a living faith and a pure worship. And by this means, much more than by their re-settlement in the land of Canaan, taken by itself, was it in their power to bend the current of men's views into the right channel, and to prepare the way for the diffusion of Christianity.

That the Jews really employed the power and the opportunities thus placed at their command to the extent they might have done, it is impossible to believe; and yet, that they did so to a very considerable extent, is put beyond a doubt by the records of New Testament Scripture itself. We see plainly enough that it was not so much the people living in Jerusalem or Judea, as those belonging to the regions already men-

tioned, who chiefly contributed to the establishment
of the Christian Church in the world. Wherever
Paul and the first heralds of the gospel went, they
found at every influential position a nucleus of devout
Jews and proselytes from the Gentiles, ready to hail
the tidings of salvation, and erect the standard of the
cross. Had these preparatory elements been wanting
—had the gospel of Jesus been left to make its way
through the dense heathenism of the ancient world
without the help of such persons in the more important places—it would doubtless have succeeded in the
end, but it would probably have taken ages to effect
what in less than one was actually accomplished.
For, in the short space of thirty years after the death
of Christ, we find that his religion had spread, not
only through Judea, Galilee, and Samaria, but also
through the numerous districts of Asia Minor, through
Greece and the islands of the Ægean Sea, the sea-coast
of Africa, and had extended itself to Rome and to
Italy. And at the close of little more than a century,
Justin Martyr boldly affirms, that "there was not a
nation, either Greek or Barbarian, or of any other
name, amongst whom prayers and thanksgivings are
not offered to the Father and Creator of the universe
in the name of the crucified Jesus.*

It is true that the greater portion of the Jews, and
some also of the proselytes, every where offered the
most determined opposition to Christianity. But it

---

* See Paley's Evidence, Part II., ch. 9, where much more to
the same purpose is to be found.

is not the less true, that there was always a spiritual
portion who became its zealous adherents, and who,
by the diffusion of the knowledge of God as disclosed
in Old Testament Scripture, had already, amid the
declining influence of heathenism, done much to pre-
dispose the minds of men for the blessed realities of the
gospel. They had not only witnessed for the truth of
God among the idolatrous nations, but had been also
so active and successful in the propagation of the
truth, as to incur many a taunt from heathens on the
subject, as well as to receive the approving testimony
of their own historian.* And as it was by means of
their dispersion that they were thus enabled to operate so extensively in the great centres of heathenism,

* Josephus says in Apion II., c. 36 : "We choose not to imitate
the institutions of other people, but we willingly embrace all that
will follow ours." In the 20th book of his Antiquities, he gives
an account of the conversion of an entire people, those of Adia-
bene, to the Jewish faith; and in his Wars, vii. c. 3, § 3, he says
of the Jews at Antioch, that they were "continually bringing a
great number of Greeks to their religion," and incidentally reports of Damascus, ii. c. 20, § 2, that nearly all the women there
were devoted to the Jewish religion. In regard to heathen
authors, Horace, for example, Sat. l. i. 4, alludes to the Jews as
the very personification of active and energetic zeal in constrain-
ing others to be of their way. Seneca too, as quoted by Augus-
tine, De Civ. Dei, l. vi. c. 11, speaks of the Jewish religion as
having been received every where, and adds, "the conquered have
given laws to the conquerors" (victi victoribus legis dederunt);
thus partly and in the noblest sense executing the vengeance
which, according to Ps. cxlix., they were to practise among the
heathen. This subject, however, has not yet been thoroughly in-
vestigated; but what has been said is sufficient for our present
purpose.

and to break up the fallow-ground for the seed of the gospel, the event itself of the dispersion should not be regarded by any means as an unmingled evil; it was an evil only in the first instance, but was both designed and overruled by God for a higher good than could otherwise have been attained. Their partial separation from Canaan and scattering among the nations, proved but another and more effectual way of securing the grand end for which most of all they had been at first planted in the land of promise.

Surely, when we reflect on all these things—when we see how wonderfully God had planned his operations in providence, contemplating the end from the beginning—how even, when thwarting the desires of his servant Jonah, he was still taking the most effectual method of promoting the objects which Jonah had chiefly at heart—and how he was at the same time lighting the way to operations and results such as Jonah had probably never so much as dreamt of—it well becomes us to exclaim in humble adoration with the apostle, " O the depth of the riches both of the wisdom and knowledge of God! how unsearchable are his judgments, and his ways past finding out! For who hath known the mind of the Lord? or who hath been his counsellor? or who hath first given to him, and it shall be recompensed to him again? For of him, and through him, and to him are all things, to whom be glory for ever. Amen."

CHAPTER X

THE reflections naturally growing out of the life and labours of Jonah, have already, for the most part, been suggested in connexion with the several topics that have successively engaged our attention. But there are, besides, some additional reflections, which a review of the whole is fitted to suggest, and with which, very briefly illustrated, we shall sum up our meditations on the subject.

1. The first we shall mention is the warning furnished by the remarkable history we have surveyed, to beware of allowing expected results to interfere with present and pressing obligations. For the most part these run into each other, and the obligation to enter upon and prosecute a definite course of labour, usually arises from our being charged with the working out of a certain beneficial result. In the duties of everyday life, and the walks of common usefulness and philanthropy, this is almost invariably the case— the good to be aimed at and secured lies before us, perfectly within our reach, if the proper means be

employed—and the faithful and diligent application of
such means, is just the discharge of the obligation that
rests upon us.

There are circumstances, however, not unfrequently
occurring in providence, in which there is not this
apparent harmony between the present and the future.
It sometimes happens, as with Jonah, that the obligation to take a certain course of action seems to
point in one direction for its result, while the result
to be actually attained is very different, and in the
first instance entirely opposite. And when such circumstances do arise, we must be careful to avoid
Jonah's error, which led to so much that was painful
in experience, as well as to what was wrong in behaviour; we must endeavour to have our course shaped,
and our wills also directed by the felt obligations
under which we lie, rather than by desired or anticipated results. The prophet Isaiah readily undertook,
on the occasion of his obtaining a vision of the divine
glory in the temple, to go as the Lord's messenger to
the people ; he exclaimed, " Here am I, send me "—
and yet the result he was presently taught to expect,
was the reverse of what he was bound to aim at accomplishing. The path of duty remained the same,
though the anxieties and labours to which it called
him were doomed from the outset to comparative
fruitlessness and general disappointment. And a
greater than Isaiah, our forerunner and pattern in all
spiritual excellence, the Lord Jesus Christ, was never
moved from the rectitude of his course, by the clear

foresight he possessed of the unsatisfactory and mournful results in which it was immediately to issue, but continued faithfully to do the will of his Father in heaven, and to execute the work given him to do, not less than if all were yielding to his wishes.

The Lord may render it manifest to the consciences of his people, that they ought to pursue a certain line of active service for the good of a neighbour, or the society in which they dwell, while still possibly the desired result may seem very doubtful, and in the issue may be found absolutely unattainable. But by the former alone should their views of duty be regulated, and their efforts in its discharge guided, for with that more immediately is their responsibility connected; and, in regard even to the results that may ultimately be made to arise from their course, these may possibly depend far less on any good immediately secured, than on the faith and patience, or even the sufferings and disappointments, which may have attended their efforts to realize it. The good that discovers itself in their example of self-sacrificing and devoted labour, may do more for the cause of righteousness than could have been accomplished by the good they were intent on achieving by their exertions, and even present defeat may be the necessary prelude to success of another and more important kind. Let but the path of present duty be made clear to us, and nothing of a collateral or contingent nature should be allowed to turn us aside; that is for us the will of God, and whatever may be the success of our course as regards the immediate objects in view, by the faithful prosecution of the course itself, the name of God is magnified and the interests of righteousness advanced.

2. Another reflection furnished by the life and labours of Jonah, respects the spheres of greatest usefulness for the servants of God, and admonishes them to watch in regard to these the leadings of providence, rather than give way to their own desires and inclinations. The field in which they are destined to reap most fruit, may possibly not be the one which they are themselves disposed to choose—it may not even be that which has received the largest share in their prayers and personal application. As generally " the times of men are before appointed by God, and the bounds of their habitations are set," so in particular his most faithful and honoured servants are often shut up by him into peculiar, and by themselves entirely unsought channels of usefulness. Jonah by no means stands alone in having accomplished, by what might in some sense be regarded as a few incidental efforts, greatly more than he was honoured to do by the regular labours of his prophetical calling. The field in which his chief success was won, though he himself knew it not, was precisely that for which he was peculiarly qualified; there his spiritual gifts and his singular experiences found the soil in which they were fitted to produce their most powerful influence. And, as many labourers in the Lord's vineyard know as little beforehand as he did what is the particular

province for which they are most peculiarly adapted, they should keep their eye awake to the indications of God's hand, and should hold themselves ready to cultivate such portions as promise under his grace to yield the largest increase to their labours.

The consideration now mentioned is one also that applies in great measure to the different kinds of spiritual labour. Men are not always themselves the best judges of the department of service by which they can do most to glorify God, any more than of the particular stations they can most successfully occupy. And some special turn of providence, not uncommonly one that in its first aspect carries an unpropitious appearance, has often been employed by God to give that direction to their powers of service, which was to render them, much beyond their own immediate expectations, benefactors to the Church or the world. It was certainly a frowning providence which threw the apostle Paul into chains, and suspended for upwards of two years his public exertions in the cause of the gospel; but to that very suspension we owe not a few of his epistles, which were called forth by the circumstances connected with his imprisonment; so that the Church of Christ only suffered, through the adverse turn of affairs, a partial and temporary deprivation of his services, that the generations to come might be more abundantly supplied with the means of spiritual life and nourishment. Nor can we doubt —the records of the past have supplied too many proofs of it—that the most fruitful exertions in the

service of God have often, in like manner, owed their
origin to what were in the first instance cross currents
in providence—currents, however, purposely raised by
God to give a direction and an impulse to gifts which
might otherwise have remained comparatively dor-
mant and fruitless, but which have thus found the
occasion that was to draw them forth into the most
vigorous and profitable exercise.

In such directing and controlling movements on
the part of God, there always appears a manifestation of his divine power and sovereignty; and in
their fitness to keep alive a practical sense of this in
the world, there is doubtless to be found one main
reason of their employment. They are among the
more evident and conspicuous ways by which he con-
strains us to feel the presence and the might of his
arm, which can turn at will the hearts of men and the
events of providence into such channels as may be
most conducive to his own glory and the interests of
his kingdom. Thus also he shows his thoughts to be
immeasurably above man's thoughts, seeing the end
from the beginning, and by his clear foresight and
wise direction timeously preventing the evils that
would arise from the narrow and short-sighted policy
of his creatures. And thus, finally, he maintains in
providence a perpetual testimony to the truth, that it
belongs to him at once to open up paths for sowing
the seed of the everlasting gospel and to bless the seed
sown; so that, as there can be no increase if he with-
holds his hand from working, the increase, on the other

hand, shall become even an hundred-fold when he comes near with the more special operations of his grace.

3. A third reflection that naturally grows out of the review of Jonah's history, is the benefit which may be derived, both for direction in duty and for the profitable study of his word and ways, from a connected and orderly view of his dispensations. Had Jonah been able to take such a comprehensive view of God's purpose at first in sending him to Nineveh, and afterwards in sparing the city, how readily would his perplexities have vanished, and his heart have acquiesced in the counsel and appointment of God! This book also, which contains the record of his mission to Nineveh, when viewed in the light now suggested, has proved to be not such a mere episode in prophecy as it is apt to appear on a hasty glance, and when considered by itself. There are, we have seen, great principles developing themselves here, common to this with a large portion of the prophetic word; and the transactions which it reports to have taken place, however singular in some respects, were still important links in the great chain of operations, by which God carried forward his schemes of providence, and brought one part into fit connexion with another.

Nothing in God's dispensations falls out at random, or is intended to stand by itself isolated and alone. All are parts of a great system, which they are wisely contrived to advance, and which is still proceeding, even amid seeming hindrances and irregularities. We may not always be able to discern the central thread which connects the parts with the whole, but we should always endeavour to do so, and should at least bear in mind that such a thread exists in the eye of God, whether we can discern it or not. It is no more than might be expected, considering that we now know but in part, that there should be apparent anomalies both in God's word and ways—things starting up at intervals which we are compelled from the imperfection of our knowledge to regard as strange and singular, or even as cross and adverse; yet it may go far in many cases to smooth these roughnesses, whether in the way of scriptural interpretation or of practical duty, to view them as far as possible in connexion with the greater principles of God's revealed truth, and the higher ends of his government. Let us beware of judging God in such things by feeble sense, or of measuring by the narrow limits of our own discernment the purposes and operations of One whose understanding is infinite. Let us especially beware of exalting some particular object, which circumstances may have contributed to render peculiarly prominent in our view, out of its proper place, and acting as if it alone should be made account of, while other objects may be present to the mind of God of still greater moment, to which it stands only in a relation of subservience. Let our prayer be that of Paul for Timothy, that " the Lord may give us understanding in all things," so as neither, by viewing his procedure in a contracted and partial light, to misinterpret his dealings nor to stumble at his dispensations.

4. Finally, we are taught here the salutary lesson, that whenever and wherever God is pleased to manifest of his grace and goodness, it is our part to acknowledge and rejoice in the manifestation. It may possibly be done through instruments that we should not have expected to be peculiarly honoured, or in regions which are in a manner cut off from our sympathies and regards. That such showers of blessing should descend there, while scarcely a drop falls where our desires and efforts are mainly engaged, may often appear strange, and may even be felt to be mortifying, as if what were given to the one were somehow withheld from the other. But this is to judge after the flesh. The Spirit of the Lord is not straitened, and what he bestows on one corner of the vineyard is not given at the expense of another—it is rather designed to awaken a desire and expectation for like gifts of grace, where they have not yet been received, and to give manifest proof to all of God's infinite power and goodness. If his eye, therefore, should be good toward any, far be it from us to cherish an evil eye—let us rather view with thankfulness the benevolent working of his hand; and what St Paul said of the preaching of the gospel at Rome, even by unworthy instruments, let us still more say of the goodness of God in the salvation of men wherever it appears, " I therein do rejoice, yea, and will rejoice."

SUPPLEMENTARY REMARKS

PART I

ON THE QUOTATIONS MADE BY PROPHETS FROM THE
WRITINGS OF EARLIER PROPHETS AND SERVANTS OF
GOD.

THE quotations here referred to are not such as
avowedly make mention of the earlier revelations of
God, but those silently adopted by a later prophet,
and given forth as part of the Spirit's utterances by
himself—what may be called *unacknowledged quotations*. Jonah's prayer, we took occasion to notice in
Chapter IV., was to a large extent made up of such
quotations from the Book of Psalms; and in the circumstances in which he was then placed, it was quite
natural that he should have thus adopted the recorded
experiences of former saints, rather than given vent
to his feelings in expressions altogether his own.
We say this, however, on the twofold supposition,
that the psalms from which the passages are taken

were already in existence and familiarly known to
the Church of God, and that a prophet, or inspired
man generally, stood on the same level with other
believers in matters of personal faith and experience.
On the first of these points, very little requires to be
said by way of supplement; for, though the interpreters of the Rationalist school have often ascribed some
of the psalms employed by the prophet to an age
much posterior to Jonah's, a more sober, and at the
same time more profound, criticism now contends for
their being productions of David and his contemporaries, so that they must have been in the hands of
the Church and people of God centuries before the
time of Jonah.

I feel it quite unnecessary to enter into any de-
tailed proof of this, as persons who are curious on
the subject can easily have their minds satisfied by
consulting the Introductions of Hengstenberg to the
several psalms referred to in connexion with the
prayer of Jonah. In the work of Hengstenberg there
is to be found a much more acute and discriminating
examination of the authorship of the different psalms
than has yet been made, either in this country or on
the Continent; and his conclusions perfectly agree
with what is implied in Jonah respecting the age of
the psalms leant on by that prophet. A recent
author, however (Krahmer), has dragged in two other
psalms, besides those indicated in Chap. IV., as having
been used in the composition of Jonah's prayer; viz.,
Ps. lxxvii. 3, for Jonah ii. 7, first clause, and Ps.

cxvi. 17, 18, for Jonah ii. 10. These two psalms certainly appear to have been composed at a period considerably later than the age of Jonah; and if any portions of his prayer had been derived from them, the conclusion might, with some appearance of truth, have been drawn, that it was not composed by Jonah himself, but by some later hand. This is the inference which Krahmer draws, and which he is particularly anxious to establish. But he builds without any solid foundation; for there is no just reason to suppose that these psalms were in the eye of the prophet, or of the person who composed this prayer; and the person who can prefer Ps. lxxvii. 3, to Ps. cxlii. 3 (a psalm of David), as the original from which the first clause of Jonah ii. 7, was borrowed, appears so manifestly to be labouring under some perverting bias, that his views on such a point may safely be left to themselves. Those who can compare the Hebrew text will more readily perceive the force of what we say.

In regard to the other point—that a prophet stood on the same level with other men in matters of personal faith and experience—there is also little room for diversity of opinion among those who are acquainted with the Word of God; for however the Spirit may have acted upon the prophets, when supernaturally conveying to their minds direct messages of God, or disclosing visions of coming events, they were plainly left in all ordinary matters to the guidance of those views and principles which belonged

to them in common with the people of God. Nor
have we any ground for supposing that their prophetical gift should have tended to raise them above
the condition of other men of faith, any more than
was done by the miraculous powers of Christ and the
apostles, who, while continually rescuing others from
the most overwhelming evils, were still themselves
subject to all the troubles, vicissitudes, and dangers
of life.   There was, indeed, a moral necessity for the
circumstance, in respect alike to the earlier and the
later messengers of God.   The same law which requires now that the treasure of the gospel should be
committed to earthen vessels, and ministered by those
who themselves need and receive the blessings of salvation, rather than by angelic beings, who belong to
a higher sphere, required also that the prophet who
bore God's message of old to the people should be a
man of like passions with themselves—exposed to the
same snares and temptations—and with the same
light, the same grace, at command, should have been
left to find, on grounds equally open to them, his
direction in duty and his consolation in trouble.
There could not otherwise have been that sympathy
between the bearers and the receivers of the message,
which in all ordinary circumstances forms an essential element to success, and which is necessary to
constitute the teachers the true guides and forerun-
ners of the taught.   So much was this the case with
the prophets, that, even in regard to the full meaning
and proper application of their predictions, they ap-

pear, sometimes at least, to have had little or no advantage over their hearers; they, too, had " to search what .or what manner of time the Spirit of Christ which was in them did signify."—(1 Pet. i. 10.) We cannot therefore be surprised that Jonah, like an ordinary believer, should have been so much indebted to the experiences of saints in former times; the less so when we reflect that Jesus, who was more than a prophet, who had the Spirit even without measure, and who perfectly knew the will of the Father, is represented to have looked for direction and support in the season of temptation, and for strength and consolation in the hour of suffering, precisely as Jonah had done before him, to the earlier manifestations of God's truth and the recorded experiences of believers in other times.

Indeed, David himself, in his later psalms, appears to have sometimes made as free a use of his earlier ones, as was done by Jonah of the psalms he found suitable to his condition in trouble. Take as an example Ps. cxliii., of which Hengstenberg has said : " It is almost wholly composed of the sounds of complaint, supplication, and hope, which had already been uttered in the earlier psalms of David, and had sunk deep into the heart. These clear brooks were drawn from all sides into the channel of this smooth-flowing psalm, which was designed to provide refreshment for the fainting souls of David's race during future times of oppression. With so much of dependence (on former productions), the psalm still

bears throughout the character of originality, not
merely where the dependence ceases, but also in the
dependent passages themselves—in the thoughtful
and artificial manner of their collocation, which could
only have proceeded from the person out of whose
breast the utterances originally welled forth." We
see the same dependence and the same originality in
the prayer of Jonah.

But persons only moderately versed in the study
of Old Testament scripture are aware, that passages
are often taken by one prophet from another, relating
to other matters than those which belong to personal
faith and experience—passages which may justly be
considered as among the more peculiar utterances of
the prophetic spirit. For example, the remarkable
prophecy in Isaiah ii. 1–4, about the exaltation of
the mountain of the Lord's house above the hills,
and the flowing of all nations to it, is almost literally
repeated by Micah iv. 1–3; and in so peculiar a
delineation of gospel times, it is impossible to doubt
that the one prophet must have adopted as his own
the prediction of the other. To say nothing of the
various references which are made in future prophetical writings to the inspired effusions of Balaam—
such as Micah vi. 5, or Hab. i. 3, 13 (where a reference is plain in the original to Numb. xxiii. 10)—
we have, in Jer. xlviii. 45, an obvious quotation from
Numb. xxiv. 17, accompanied, however, with a slight
alteration, evidently for the purpose of rendering the
fundamental passage in Numbers more plain; for

though the alteration in the Hebrew is much less than in the translation, yet it has the effect of substituting for "destroying all the children of Sheth" (tumult), "the crown of the head of the tumultuous ones." There are many similar examples in Jeremiah, who, more than any other prophet, adopts the language of his predecessors; but, in particular, his prophecy upon Edom, in ch. xlix. 7-22, is in great part a repetition of the first verses of Obadiah's prophecy; as, again, various ideas and expressions in Obadiah are evidently taken from the last chapter of Joel—(compare, for example, Obad. v. 11, "They cast lots upon Jerusalem," with Joel iii. 3, "And they have cast lots for my people;" Obad. v. 15, "Thy reward shall return upon thine own head," the same as Joel iii. 4, 7; Obad. v. 17, "And upon Zion shall be deliverance," Joel ii. 32, &c.)

Such appropriations by one prophet of the writings of another, may possibly appear to some hardly consistent with that lofty and ecstatic condition to which they justly apprehend the prophets to have been raised, when "speaking as they were moved by the Holy Ghost." It may seem to impart to such portions of the prophetic word an appearance of art and labour, and to assimilate them in human literature to the productions of those who endeavour to make up for the want of original genius by borrowing the ideas and expressions of more gifted intellects. Nothing less, indeed, than this is the misapplication that has been made of the circumstance in question by a class

of authors, who always seem to feel as if they lighted
on a valuable discovery when they meet with any thing
that tends to depreciate the character of Scripture, and
to stamp it with something like human imperfection.
The existence of quotations in a portion of prophetic
scripture, is, in the eye of such persons, the indication
simply of a low and defective spirit, and is not uncommonly appealed to as the clear proof of a degenerate age, when the sacred penmen attempted little
more than a few compilations from the original sources.

This, we need hardly say, is an entirely false view
of the subject; neither is there any just reason for
regarding the existence of such borrowed passages
as inferring the least diminution of the Spirit's influence, or any constraint on his movements in the soul.
For the prophetic utterances, it must be remembered,
like the Psalms of David, were usually made public
as soon as delivered, and added to the existing testimony of God; they became part of the sacred trea-
sury of the Church; and thenceforth formed, not only
as to the thoughts expressed in them, a portion of
revealed truth, but also, as to the very expressions
employed, a kind of hallowed tongue in which to declare the same thoughts anew, as often as occasion
might require them to be again uttered. Have we
not the confirmation of experience to this, perpetually
recurring? When a man is much under the power
of the Spirit, do not his thoughts on divine things instinctively, as it were, run in scriptural channels, and
clothe themselves, when he speaks, in the very lan-

guage of inspiration? The more powerfully the Spirit works within, giving spontaneous birth to spiritual thoughts and feelings, the more readily do they take this scriptural direction; as we already see in the apostles, when, on being released from the first attempts of persecuting rulers, and filled with the Holy Ghost, they poured forth their hearts to God with one accord, in the very words that had been indited centuries before by the hand of David in the second psalm (Acts iv. 23–27). St Paul was in the highest sense a chosen vessel, and both spake and wrote " in the words which the Holy Ghost teacheth;" yet he ever makes the freest use of the earlier scriptures, and sometimes, as when enjoining the duty of forgiveness of injuries (Rom. xii. 19-21), contents himself with taking up and reiterating the testimony of former times. And how often does the apostle Peter throughout his first epistle address to the New Testament Church, as from himself, passages that were originally addressed by other servants of God to the Church of the Old Testament? Yet such passages are as much the communications of the Holy Spirit on their second, as they were on their first appearance; for the purpose of God required that a fresh utterance should be given to the sentiments they expressed, and the original form of expression was on many accounts the best that could be chosen.

Besides, there were some ends of a more special kind to be served by the references and quotations from one prophet to another. For these form so many landmarks in the field of ancient prophecy, indicating the relation of one portion to another; they are so many links in the chain of God's testimony, connecting the earlier with the later, always betokening the prior existence of the earlier, reiterating anew its tidings, and sometimes also throwing light on its import. "The Old Testament prophets," says a learned and able writer,* "form a continuous body; they are members of an unbroken, connected chain; one perpetually reaches forth the hand to another. The later prophets had always either heard or read the prophecies of the earlier, which had made a deep and lasting impression on their minds. And when the Spirit of God came upon a prophet himself, and irresistibly impelled him to prophesy (Am. iii. 8), it naturally came to pass that here and there, sometimes more, sometimes less, he clothed what had been imparted to him by the prophetic spirit in the words of one or more of the prophets he had heard or read; that the words of his prophetical forerunner, cleaving to his memory, formed part of the materials of utterance of which the Spirit of God availed himself. Hence also it happened, that the later prophet entered into the prophetical views of the earlier, and, in the power of the prophetic spirit descending on him from above, and working in his soul, either confirmed them anew by a second promulgation, or expanded them further, and brought them to comple-

* Der Prophet Obadia, ausgelegt von Carl Paul Caspari, pp. 21, 22.

tion. For the most part, the coincidence in thought and expression go together in the prophets."

Another able writer on prophecy, and the friend and coadjutor of the author just quoted, has followed up these observations by similar remarks in his introduction to the third chapter of the prophet Habakkuk—a chapter which is not less distinguished by the vein of originality that pervades it, than by the free use which it also makes of some of the earlier portions of Scripture, especially of the 77th Psalm. "With the inspired penman in general," says Delitzsch, "and with the prophet in particular, simply from his being a living member of the spiritual body, there was formed an internal storehouse out of the substance of former revelations, which had entered into his inmost spiritual life and become part of it—revelations which sunk so deep into the memory and the heart of every well-instructed Israelite, that as he necessarily acted under their influence in the formation and utterance of his thoughts, so, when writing, he would involuntarily make use of the older expressions, which already bore upon them a divine impress. Besides, the prophet could no otherwise be the organ and bearer of a divine revelation, than by sacrificing every thing of a selfish kind, therefore all ambitious strivings after originality, that he might surrender himself to the influence of God; which influence was twofold, partly *mediate*, in respect to what had already been produced, partly *immediate*, yet even then working

in close connexion with the word that had previously
been spoken. The conformity of the new, which
germinated from the mind of the prophet, with the
old, which had been imported into his mind, was
necessitated indeed by the circumstance, that the
revelation in its *organic* development could only
present the aspect of something new, in so far as it
assumed the old in order to confirm and still further
expand it, without the possibility, in the *process* of
development, which proceeds from God, the *Unchangeable*, of running into opposition to what had
gone before. This unison is just the seal of divine
revelation, as the work of one and the same spirit
operating in the workshops of many individuals." *

It is not unimportant to add, that while the mutual
connexion and inter-dependence now noticed between
the writings of the prophets, is fitly regarded as the
appropriate seal of the unity of the Spirit, from
whom as a whole they proceeded, it also forms a
concealed evidence of the genuineness and authen-
ticity of the several parts. Great efforts have been
made by modern criticism to bring down the age of
some of the more remarkable prophecies to a period
when the events foretold had either already come to
pass, or were so near that they might have been
descried as certain by natural sagacity. And most
important aid has been derived, in proving the real
age and authorship of the prophecies in question,

* Der Prophet Habakuk, ausgelegt von Franz Delitzsch, pp.
118, 119.

from the dependence manifested in them upon earlier Scriptures. By this species of criticism, the two authors above mentioned especially have done essential service to the cause of truth in the works cited from, and by Caspari in another work on Isaiah's prophecies recently published.

PART II

WE have already in Chapter VII., when treating of
the sudden change in the divine procedure toward
Nineveh, laid it down as a principle necessary to be
kept in mind, in the interpretation of those prophecies
which possess the nature of threatenings or promises,
that they must be understood in connexion with a
certain spiritual condition, on the part of those to
whom they were addressed, so that they shall continue applicable, in their original import and destination,
only so long as that condition lasts. The manner of
dealing with Nineveh was a palpable proof of this in
providence, just as the passages quoted from Jeremiah
and Ezekiel were a clear and emphatic assertion of
the principle itself, as one essentially connected with
the moral rectitude of God's procedure. Such prophecies ought consequently to be regarded in the first
instance, and chiefly, as revelations of the *righteous
character* of God in his dealings with men, and not

simply or directly as pledges thrown out beforehand, by which afterwards to test and verify his omniscience. It seems to me of great importance to keep this principle steadily in view, as well for arriving at a correct interpretation of a large portion of the prophetic word, as for giving the things belonging to it the same relative place in our estimation which they hold in the testimony of God.   And for the purpose of bringing out these points more fully, and establishing the principle itself, as I trust, on a sure foundation, I have resolved to give the subject here a somewhat closer and more lengthened consideration.

The desire of meeting the sceptical tendencies of modern times with a sort of demonstrative evidence of the truth of Scripture, has to some extent diverted the course of inquiry in this field into a wrong channel.   For it has led nearly all our recent writers on ancient prophecy to make the truth that appears in the prediction, as compared with the fulfilment, the almost exclusive object of their investigations. Prophecies respecting the people and states of former times have thus come to possess chiefly a polemical interest; and are seldom regarded in any other light than as serving, by the proof they afford of divine foresight, to strengthen the foundations of the faith, and put to silence the ignorance of foolish men.   Nor can there be any room with enlightened believers to doubt, that the comparison of the word of prophecy with the events of providence, so as thereby to evince the unfailing certainty of God's declarations, is *one* of the uses that ought to be made of the prophetic word by those who have the advantage of being able to place the prediction side by side with the events to which it pointed. We find the apostles at the beginning of the gospel plying this argument with their countrymen—constantly appealing to the Scriptures which had spoken before of Christ, as conclusive evidence of the divine character and mission of Jesus of Nazareth, in whose eventful history they had received so exact, and yet so unexpected a fulfilment. And the Lord himself by Isaiah challenges men's undoubting confidence in his word, on the special ground of his having foretold what had already taken place: "Behold the former things are come to pass, and new things do I declare; before they spring forth I tell you of them."

It is plain, therefore, that this is one use to be made of the prophetical Scriptures, and consequently one of the ends God had in view in causing such Scriptures to be indited. But it by no means follows, that such is either the only or the primary view that ought to be taken of them; and if it is not, then serious evils cannot fail to arise from its being alone brought into consideration. What strikes us, indeed, at the first glance into the subject, is the low aspect to which men's minds are thus familiarized respecting a portion of God's revelations—as if the grand question turned simply on their truthfulness; whether the infinite and eternal Being, who speaks in them, were really entitled to the belief and confidence of

his creatures? or whether it be in truth the same
God that rules in providence who also speaks in the
Word? That he has so spoken there, as at the same
time to furnish many clear and infallible proofs of
his power and godhead, is undoubtedly true; but this
only incidentally, and as growing out of the very
nature of his communications, which, in accomplishing their other and more immediate ends, could not
fail also to bear witness to the divine perfections and
prerogatives of Him from whom they proceeded.
The Bible is still throughout, and nowhere indeed
more directly than in its promises of good and
threatenings of evil, essentially *moral* in its tone, and
in the leading purport of its communications from
above. God does not present himself there to men,
as if he sought to convince them *that* he is; but
rather as wishing to show them *what* he is, what are
the elements of his character and the principles of
his government; and in connexion with these, what,
not so much he *can* do, as what he *will* or will *not*
do, in conformity with the righteousness which must
regulate every step of his procedure. In short, it is
the moral, and not the natural attributes of God,
which those revelations of his mind and will are
always designed primarily and chiefly to exhibit to
the view of his creatures; and to invert this order in
regard to any portion of them—to represent them as
principally valuable on account of the exhibitions
they contain of God's existence, or power, or
omniscience, is substantially to bring them down to

the region of nature, and to view them apart from
the great ends for which they were more immediately
given.   Hence, it quite naturally happened, that in
the hands of those who were wont to consider the
prophecies and miracles of Scripture in the light
merely of evidences (the one of God's prescience, the
other of his power), the religion itself of the Bible
degenerated into a kind of refined deism, having to
do chiefly with the existence of God, and the natural
powers and attributes of his being.

There are no doubt, as was noticed in the chapter
already referred to, certain intimations of coming
events in prophecy, which may justly be regarded as
of an absolute and unconditional nature, and which
so peculiarly demand an exact fulfilment, that we
can scarcely avoid making the correspondence between the prediction and the reality our primary
subject of inquiry.   But those prophecies which
respect the destinies of certain states and people—
which are pregnant with evil or with good to those
interested in their tidings—bring us of necessity into
direct contact with the principles of God's righteous
government.   The good and the evil in such cases
are never capriciously announced, but always stand
connected with moral grounds; they are just pre-
intimations of God's mind toward man, considered as
in the one case deserving of punishment, and in the
other as fit subjects of blessing.   And it is as if one
would dissociate God's working in providence from his
moral perfections, when such things are regarded in the

light merely of physical necessities—as things that must develop themselves in a particular region at any rate, whatever the spiritual condition of its inhabitants—as arbitrary exhibitions of his prescience and his power!

But this is only one reason against taking the kind of prophecies referred to in so absolute and independent a sense, and viewing them mainly with an eye to their truthfulness. There is another and still weightier one—one that bears directly on the meaning and interpretation of the prophecies themselves. For in the messages God gave to the prophets concerning the kingdoms and people of ancient times, there is for the most part a good as well as an evil held out in prospect. There are in fact two lines of prophecy respecting them, which point in two precisely opposite directions, and do so plainly because the people or kingdoms referred to are contemplated in two different and contrary relations—in the one viewed as proper subjects of blessing, in the other of cursing. Take as an example Babylon, which first comes upon the stage of sacred history in the time of Hezekiah, and in a friendly relation, among the worldly powers that sent ambassadors and brought presents to Hezekiah after the signal overthrow of the Assyrian army before the gates of Jerusalem. In this acknowledgment of the Lord's interposition for the good of his covenant people, the prophets descried a sign of the submission of the heathen to God's authority, and their ultimate incorporation with the inhabitants of Zion. This view is presented

in Ps. lxxxvii. (as it had previously been in Ps.
lxviii), where Babylon, as well as Egypt, Tyre,
Philistia, and Ethiopia, appear in vision to the prophet
among those that know God, and have their names
written down among the living in Jerusalem. And
this prophey of course, in so far as it was destined to
receive its fulfilment in Babylon, must have had its
accomplishment in the past; for by Babylon, so introduced, it is impossible to understand any thing
but the gigantic worldly power which was then beginning to rear its head in the north, and in that respect
has long since finally perished.

But when we turn to Isaiah, we find Babylon presented to our view in an entirely different relation—
one that takes for its starting-point the undue elation
which the message from Babylon raised in the mind
of Hezekiah. This was eyed by the prophetic Spirit
in Isaiah as but one of the symptoms of that fatal
tendency to lean on the powers of the world which
had already provoked the displeasure of God, and
was destined by and by to draw down the severe visitations of his wrath; and the prophet took occasion
from it, not only to foretell the temporary triumph
of Babylon over Judah (ch. xxxix. 5-7), but also
from that, as a new starting-point, went on to announce (in ch. xiii. and xiv. and elsewhere) the certainty of Babylon's coming downfal, and her complete and final desolation. Rightly understood—that
is, with a due regard to the different relations contemplated, and the corresponding difference in the

points of view taken—this latter delineation is no way inconsistent with the former; for the one views Babylon as brought to see the insufficiency of her idols and her pleasures, and coming to seek salvation and blessing from the God of Zion—while in the other she is contemplated as the proud rival of Zion, and the sworn enemy of the cause and kingdom that had their centre there. It was to be understood of itself, that the one line of prophecy would meet and qualify the other, whenever a change in the spiritual condition of the people might call for a corresponding change in the dealing of God toward them; and we can scarcely doubt, it was to allow scope for the promised good being sought and experienced, that the threatened evil was made to develop itself so slowly. For though in the future history of Babylon the doom of woe is what chiefly rises into notice, yet we are not to suppose that this alone took effect; in the times of the captivity, through the instrumentality of Daniel and the faithful portion of the Jews, many were doubtless led to acknowledge and serve the living God. Especially would this be the case after God's hand began to execute vengeance on the pride of Babylon; and that Peter, centuries later still, should have dated his first epistle from Babylon, and sent salutations from the Church there to the brethren scattered abroad, is a clear sign how much mercy mingled with judgment, and how truly it might be said even of Babylon, " This and that man was born in Zion." There still was a blessing for her people,

which partly stayed, and, if she had known aright
the time of her visitation, might have wholly stayed
the curse from proceeding; and, in so far as any blessing did come to her, it came out of Zion.

But a still more striking example of this double
line of prophecy, and of the necessity of taking into
account the spiritual condition of the people for understanding aright the things spoken concerning them,
is furnished in the case of Edom. In the earlier
stages of Israel's history, a friendly spirit was manifested toward the children of Edom; the Lord sought
to overcome their enmity with kindness, and they
held the first place among those whom the children
of Israel were instructed to receive into the congre-
gation of the Lord.—(Deut. xxiii. 7-8). This exhibition of kindness, however, failed in great measure to
produce the desired effect; the spirit of enmity still
slumbered in Edom, ready to break forth into acts of
hostility whenever a suitable occasion presented itself;
and in the later periods of Israel's history, when the
kingdom of Judah was verging to ruin, and the
mighty empires of the north were rising to the ascendant, the Edomites became the most bitter and malignant of all the adversaries of Judah, and betook
to the most cruel methods of gratifying their revenge.
—(Joel iii. 19; Obad. 10-14; Amos i. 11-12; Ps.
cxxxvii. 7). Hence, as the foremost of all the enemies of the covenant people in malice and bitterness
of spirit, the Edomites came to be viewed by the Spirit of prophecy as the kind of quintessence of all ma-

lice and enmity—the heads and representatives of the
wholy army of the aliens, whose doom was to carry
along with it the downfal and destruction of every
thing that opposed and exalted itself against the
knowledge of God.   This is the view presented in
the short prophecy of Obadiah—all the heathen share
in Edom's fate: " For the day of the Lord is near
upon all the heathen; as thou hast done, it shall be
done unto thee; thy reward shall return upon thine
own head," &c.   But at still greater length, and with
images of terrific grandeur, the same view is unfolded
in the 34th chapter of Isaiah, where all the nations
of the earth are summoned together, because " the
Lord's indignation was upon them all;" while the
fury to be poured out upon them was to discharge its
violence, and rest in a manner upon the mountains of
Idumea.   It is clear that, in the precise form which
the subject here assumes, it is to a large extent an
ideal representation—clear from the very conjunction
of all the heathen with Edom, and also from the peculiar strength of the images employed, such as the
dissolving of the host of heaven, the sword of the
Lord being bathed in heaven, the mountains melt-
ing with blood, the turning of the streams into pitch,
and the dust into brimstone, which (like the ascrip-
tion of human organs and human passions to God)
seem purposely intended to guard us against under-
derstanding the words in the grossly literal sense.
The same also appears quite obvious from the relation
which Edom is represented as holding toward Israel,

and which was such, that the execution of judgment
upon the one would be the era of deliverance, joy,
and blessing to the other—the era when the controversy of Zion would be settled, and everlasting prosperity be ushered in.

The meaning of the prophecy, when stript of the
mere form and drapery in which it is clothed, is manifestly of this nature: the enmity and opposition
toward the Lord's cause and people which had
showed itself in the heathen nations, and particularly
in Edom, cannot possibly accomplish its end; it must
be visited with judgment, the more severe in executions of evil, the higher the spirit of hatred and malice has risen in the judged; insomuch that the coming evil may be regarded as concentrating itself in
Edom, the keenest of the enemies, just as the favour
and blessing of God toward his people is represented
as centring in Zion, and from that diffusing itself to
the ends of the earth. The prophecy, indeed (including the 34th and 35th chapters, which form one
piece), is a sort of recapitulation, and sums up in one
glowing delineation what had already in substance
been presented in several successive chapters. The
prophet had gone over, one by one, every people and
kingdom who acted in a spirit of rivalry or spite toward the children of the covenant, and in respect to
each had declared that their pride must be humbled,
that their glory must perish, that they must be shaken
and destroyed. And now, gathering the whole, as it
were, into one mass, bringing the contest to a single

point, with the view of more distinctly and impressively exhibiting the awful certainty of the issue, he represents the vials of divine wrath as emptying themselves in a mighty torrent upon Edom, that peace and prosperity might henceforth settle in perpetual sunshine on the seed of blessing. So that, if no other prophecy had existed regarding Edom, we should still have been bound to conclude from the evident purport of this, that it was strictly applicable to Edom only so long as it continued to be characterised by the old spirit of intense malignity and opposition to the cause and people of God. It must, therefore, have found whatever fulfilment it was properly to receive before the coming of Christ; for by that time the relation which the prediction contemplated had ceased; the Edomites had even become amalgamated with the Jews, and no longer existed as a separate people; and however the things which had been spoken, or the things which might still fall out respecting it, might bear a prospective application to other peoples and times, yet the Edomites themselves had passed out of the region in which the prophecy moved, and a different state of things had entered.*

* I profess myself utterly unable to understand how Dr Keith and other writers on prophecy can so thoroughly exclude the above considerations from their minds. They accumulate proofs from travellers of the *present* desolation of Idumea, as *simpliciter* evincing the correctness of Isaiah's prophecy, as if it had been the mere territory of Edom, the region of Idumea, God had a quarrel with, and not rather Edom as a people ("the people of his curse," as they are called in the prophecy), and the land only as connected with them. What has that land to do now, or

But Edom was also the subject of prophecies,
which spoke a very different language from those
now referred to, and which of necessity must have
sometimes qualified, and to a certain extent supplanted
the other.   Of this description is the concluding portion of Obadiah's burden, which, with all its tidings of
woe for Edom as the enemy, does not terminate without intimating, that " saviours should come up on
mount Zion to judge the mount of Esau"—which, in
other words, declares, that while salvation could only
be found in connexion with the God and people of
Zion, yet even the children of Edom would share in
its benefits ; the people of God's curse were yet to

what has it had to do for two thousand years, with the Edomites,
the peculiar enemies of God ?   Three or four centuries before
Christ, the Edomites moved up toward the south of Judea, and
what was originally the country of Moab, where, after successive
encounters, they were subdued by the Maccabees, circumcised
and incorporated with the Jewish people, so that " the house of
Esau," according to Obad. v. 18, was in a manner " devoured"
as a separate and hostile nation by the house of Judah.   And according to the same prophet, v. 19, " they of the south," that is,
the Nabathæans, an Ishmaelite race, got possession of the district
of Mount Zion, under whom the trade of the country revived,
and Petra the capital rose to great strength and prosperity.   In
process of time Christianity spread through it, and Petra became
the seat of a Christian bishop, and continued to be so till the rise
of Mahomet.   To make the terrible denunciations of Isaiah still
applicable, in their strict and proper sense, to a country which
has so completely shifted its relations, is to bring these denunciations into the region of absolute caprice—to hold them still in
force, though the very ground, we may say, of their existence is
gone !   And as we might naturally expect with a prophecy so
completely torn from its connexion, it is but scraps of fulfilment

become to a certain extent a seed of blessing; so that complete destruction, in the sense of universal and exterminating slaughter, could never have been meant. In like manner, and still more strongly, the prophet Amos, chap. ix. 12, makes mention of a time, when not only the heathen in general, but Edom in particular, should be among those over whom God's name was to be called; that is, should stand related to him, like the Jews in their best condition, as his peculiar people; for the things or people over whom God's name is called, are just those he claims as peculiarly his own. It is manifest that this exhibition of coming good for Edom

which the present state of Idumea can furnish, and an unbeliever might justly ask, Where are the rest? There are ruined cities, it is true, and wild creatures of the desert, and thorns and brambles, where palaces once stood; but (if all is to be taken in the grossly literal sense, and in respect to present times) where is the carnage of all nations that was to precede these? where the burning pitch and brimstone? where the mountains melted with blood, or the impossibility of any one passing through it? and where, above all, the people themselves, who formed the very heart and centre of Isaiah's picture? We cannot speak of God's word being verified by halves; and this prophecy, in the true sense and meaning of its delineation, has already, so far as ancient Edom was concerned, received its fulfilment. Pointing to that as an obvious and existing fact in Providence, Malachi (about 400 years B.C.) says, "I hated Esau, and laid his mountains and his heritage waste for the dragons of the wilderness." The desolation was still recent, and the Edomites, it seems, thought of repairing it; but the Lord goes on to declare the impossibility of this; Edom could never again become an independent and flourishing nation, and this is what is meant by their being appointed to perpetual desolations.

was given in anticipation of their entering into an
entirely different relation to Israel from what they
formerly held ; and that as soon as this better line
of things entered, and in the same proportion that it
did so, the threatened doom, as in the case of Nineveh, became supplanted by tokens of Divine goodness.   That this did take place to some extent, the
facts stated below leave no room to doubt ; though it
is too manifest, from the scattered notices given by
Josephus of the Edomite portion of the Jewish
nation, in the concluding drama of their history, that
the larger part, even when amalgamated with the children of Jacob, still retained their hatred to the truth
of God, and were pursued by the curse suspended
over their ungodliness.   But whether the evil or the
good was to be experienced, it must have run its
course long ago with Edom—for the people have for
ever lost their separate national existence ; and
whether the ancient territory they occupied may now
be desolate or flourishing, is of no moment as con-
cerns the prophecies that went before concerning
them.   In that respect, *actum est.*

The examples now given show clearly enough,
that those prophecies respecting the ancient nations
which contained threatenings of evil, as they always
sprung from a moral ground, the wickedness of the
people, so they depended for the amount of fulfilment
they were to receive upon the future character of
those against whom they were directed.   They revealed God's mind toward such, as embodying a

certain kind or degree of unrighteousness, and were to be understood as abiding in force only so long as this remained in operation. And how can we reasonably doubt, that the same principle equally holds in respect to those prophecies which are of an opposite kind—which contain, not threatenings of evil, but promises of good? These, too, must always virtually imply at least, if they do not expressly indicate, a certain spiritual condition on the part of those interested in the tidings; and only in the proportion that the one might be attained, could the other be intended to meet with a proper fulfilment. That this would be the case generally indeed, the Lord very clearly intimated to his people before they entered the land of Canaan, by suspending over them both a blessing and a curse—a blessing if they fulfilled the righteous ends for which they were to be planted there, and a curse if they fell into idolatry and corruption. And in one remarkable case, that of Eli, the lineal descendant of Phinehas the high priest, the Lord very strongly and emphatically set his seal to the principle in question: "Wherefore the Lord God of Israel saith, I said indeed, that thy house and the house of thy father should walk before me for ever; but now the Lord saith, Be it far from me; for them that honour me I will honour, and they that despise me shall be lightly esteemed."—1 Sam. ii. 30. God never meant that the promise should take effect any how; like all other intimations of his mind and will, it had its root in the moral nature of God; and as

the house of Eli were now acting in flagrant disregard of this, the promise formerly pledged to them of
necessity fell to the ground.

Precisely similar are many promises made at a later
period to the Jews through the prophets. "Thus
saith the Lord, after seventy years be accomplished
at Babylon, I will visit you, and perform my good
word toward you, in causing you to return to this
place. . . . And ye shall seek me, and find me,
when ye shall search (or rather, for ye shall search)
for me with all your heart. And I will be found of
you, saith the Lord; and I will turn away your
captivity, and I will gather you from all the nations,
and from all the places whither I have driven you,
saith the Lord; and I will bring you again into the
place whence I caused you to be carried away cap-
tive."—Jer. xxix. 10–14. And the word spoken by
Zechariah to the remnant who did return and settle
again at Jerusalem : "Thus saith the Lord, I am returned unto Zion, and will dwell in the midst of
Jerusalem ; and Jerusalem shall be called a city of
truth, and the mountain of the Lord of Hosts, the
holy mountain."—Zech. viii. 3. It is impossible,
by any fair construction of the words, to understand
the statements made in these prophecies of any
periods but the one of the return from Babylon, the
other of the period immediately following. And if
it is asked, When during any period of the past were
such prospects of good actually realized? when did
God so gather the children of Israel from all lands,

and himself again so dwell in Jerusalem, as to render all its habitations secure, peaceful, and holy? we reply by asking, When was the word of Jonah concerning the destruction of Nineveh in forty days verified? No future destruction of Nineveh could possibly verify that word, no more than any future gathering of the dispersed, or any future inhabitation of the Lord at Jerusalem, could verify the words spoken by these prophets respecting determinate periods in the past. The Lord stayed the execution of his threatening against Nineveh when a state of things entered to which it did not apply. In like manner, the fulfilment of the promises referred to were partly stayed by a spirit of ungodliness among the people of the Jews, first indisposing many of them to return when the call and the opportunity came to them, and then rendering it necessary for God to withhold his hand from blessing many of those who had returned. It was God's kind and gracious propensions toward them—his desire and readiness to do them good in the manner and to the extent specified in the word of promise—it was this, properly, that was indicated there—this alone that was certainly and infallibly indicated; the rest depended on the spiritual condition and behaviour of the people; and the writings of Malachi, the last of the prophets, are simply, as to their direct and immediate object, a vindication of the Lord's dealings in not bestowing as much in the way of blessing as the people thought themselves entitled to expect.

Let the character of this vindication be carefully
noted; for it proceeds entirely on the ground, that
the perverseness and obstinacy of the people had, as
it were, violently arrested the flow of divine mercy.
Throughout the whole of the book the people have
evidently in their eye the large prospects that had
been held out by the prophets immediately before, and
presently after, the captivity: they appear fretting and
complaining that these had not been realized, and
that their condition generally was poor and unsatisfactory. The prophet meets this state of feeling by
telling them that God had manifestly given them
tokens of his favour which had been withheld from
others—that, for the rest, the failure lay entirely with
themselves—that their own corruptions had rendered
an abridgement of the promised good absolutely necessary—that if they would but prove God by a sincere and faithful behaviour, they would find no want
of the promised good; while, if they persevered in
their sinful ways, matters would get worse instead of
better—they would be smitten with a curse, and not
replenished with blessing. Yet, so far from owning
that God in this was departing from his covenant
engagements, the prophet represents it as rather a
fulfilling of these; especially in ch. ii. 1-9, where ex-
postulating with a corrupt priesthood, and threatening them with the greatest displeasure and contempt
for their backslidings, he speaks of it as being done,
" that they might know that God's covenant was with
Levi;" i. e., might know how it was with him, for

what ends and purposes; so that, if these failed to be accomplished, they should justly be held responsible for the evil, and visited with chastisement.

Great misunderstanding and confusion has arisen in all ages from contemplating God's declarations in scripture from a merely natural point of view; and the same cause is now proving a most fertile source of false interpretation in prophecy. Interpreters will never see eye to eye respecting much that is there, unless they come to view it primarily and chiefly in connexion with the *moral* character and operations of Godhead. For what has been justly said (by Trench) of the miracles of scripture, that they differ essentially from apocryphal miracles, in being from their very nature witnesses of the grand moral design of their author, while the other are continually mere sports and freaks of power, having no ethical motive or meaning whatever, holds true also of the prophecies—of that class especially to which the preceding observations apply. They stand immediately connected with the moral purposes of God, and if dissociated from these, we are in danger of giving them an import and an application which they were never meant to possess.

PART III

ON CERTAIN MODERN THEORIES RESPECTING THE AUTHOR AND THE BOOK OF JONAH.

THE best antidote to error is usually the full exhibition of the truth; and if the views unfolded in the preceding pages have commended themselves to the understandings and the consciences of intelligent readers, the theories that have been propounded on the Continent for the purpose of solving the enigma, as it is called, of Jonah's marvellous history, might safely be left to themselves. Those theories, indeed, have never attained to any credit in this country, and have owed whatever countenance they have received abroad, partly to the prevalence of a sceptical turn of mind, which looks askance at every thing that wears the aspect of the miraculous, and partly to the inadequate and mistaken views that have been commonly entertained respecting the character and mission of Jonah. It is evidently difficulties proceeding from this latter source which have led Professor Stuart, in his work on the Old Testamant canon, to give only a kind of wavering dissent from some of the German

speculations on the subject, and to represent himself
as chiefly influenced by our Lord's reference to the
transactions in the book of Jonah, in adhering to their
strictly historical character.   He still regards the substance of the book as involved in inexplicable mystery.
" The mission of Jonah to a distant *heathen* country,
in his day scarcely known among the Jews, and the
mission of a man who had such a temper as Jonah,
to execute so grave a commission," are to his mind
difficulties so great, that " he does not wonder so
many interpreters should have resorted to allegory or
parable in order to explain the book."   But these
peculiarities have been quite naturally and satisfac-
torily accounted for, merely by contemplating the
subject from the right point of view, and considering
it in its proper relations; and there hence appears no
occasion or pretext for resorting to such desperate
shifts in interpretation, as would imply the historical
character of the book to be without any solid foundation.

If the *object* of the book, however, were what Professor Stuart represents, or if the view he gives of this
should come to be generally acquiesced in, I fear its
strictly historical character will be found to stand on
a very uncertain foundation.   Having announced the
problem in this respect to be one of difficult solution,
he presently asks, " What can the object be unless it
is to inculcate on the narrow-minded and bigoted
Jews (there were many such) the great truth, that
God regards the humble and penitent every where

with favour, and that even the haughty, cruel, idolatrous, and domineering heathen, in case they repent
and humble themselves, become the subjects of his
compassion and clemency, and are more acceptable
than the haughty Jew, claiming descent from Abraham, but still the devoted slave of ritual observances
and of his own evil passions?" This is precisely the
representation given of the contents of the book by the
German theorists, from whose cobwebs Mr Stuart
would fain disentangle himself, but who have been
driven chiefly by that very view of the contents to
fable and conjecture, for the purpose of more easily
explaining the circumstances it records; and it is
scarcely possible for any one consistently to hold the
same view, without letting go to some extent the historical verity of the transactions.

For, while there can be no question that there have
been many narrow-minded and bigoted Jews who
needed such an instruction, yet not when Jonah lived
in the kingdom of Israel. Never, perhaps, so little as
then, when every thing was rushing headlong for the
want of a strict adherence to the fundamental elements
of a Jewish worship, and the landmarks could
scarcely any longer be traced between the professed
disciples of Moses and the devotees of Gentile idolatry. Bigoted Judaism indeed! Devoted slaves of
ritual observances! Would that so much even of the
shadow of sound principle had prevailed to any large
extent during the dissolute period of the second Jeroboam! What the men of that generation specially

needed was, an instruction that would point altogether in the opposite direction—one that should enforce upon their depraved and senseless minds an observance of the laws and institutions of Moses, such as they had never seriously contemplated. And it was not for ages after that period, not indeed till two or three centuries subsequent to the return from Babylon, when a proud and carnal Pharisaism began to make its appearance, that those elements sprung up among the Jewish people which are supposed to have called forth the peculiar instruction conveyed by the transactions of the book of Jonah. Hence it is that the German theorists who take the view now mentioned of its object, most naturally couple with it the opinion, that the book itself is not the production of Jonah, but of some later author, who merely connected with it the name of Jonah to give a prophetical authority to the ideas he sought to impress upon his countrymen. Nor, if they were right in their premises, could we well deny the justness of their conclusion; for it never was the custom of God to institute special proceedings in providence with the view of inculcating lessons which were not properly to be required till some future period—these were always called forth by the necessities of the time, whatever ulterior designs they may also have been fitted to serve; and, had we no other view of the object of the book of Jonah than that given by Professor Stuart, we should feel constrained with the Germans to resort to the supposition of its late origin, and the chiefly ideal character of its contents.

But let us look for a little, since we *have* touched upon the subject, at the theories which have issued from those giants in theological literature, that we may see on what grounds we are called to believe the book of Jonah to be the offspring of a comparatively late age, and to be made up of fictitious representations rather than of historical facts. The writers who concur in this general idea fall into two classes, according as they belong to a more or a less extreme school of Rationalism. Those of the former class regard the book as a sheer fable without *any* historical basis, and in its narrative part of no higher authority than the myths or legends of ancient heathenism. Theories of this extravagant and obnoxious form deserve only to be treated with silent contempt, and indeed they have proved too rank productions for the soil that gave them birth. The more prevailing opinion in Germany is, that of the less extreme Rationalists, who suppose that there were certain historical data for the narrative, such as that Jonah did live and prophesy in the reign of Jeroboam II.—that he uttered some predictions in the name of Jehovah against the then rising power of Assyria—that these, however, were not to receive their fulfilment for a considerable time—that he was dissatisfied with the delay, &c. But with these shreds of an imagined historical groundwork, they consider the leading incidents of the book—the flight of Jonah to Tarshish, his being cast into the sea, his miraculous preservation in the belly of a fish, the second commission to Nineveh, the sudden conversion of the people, the wonderful growth of the plant that shaded Jonah, his displeasure at the unexpected exercise of divine mercy—these, with several minor circumstances, they consider but so many parabolical representations, which the author has woven together for the purpose of bringing more distinctly out the moral instruction which the whole was designed to impart. The instruction itself, as summed up by Krahmer, the latest and apparently one of the ablest of those who have written on the subject, includes the following particulars : " That no one, not even a prophet, must pretend to be wiser than God, and set himself in opposition to the divine will, otherwise punishment is sure to overtake him ; that the fear of God and implicit obedience to his will is the first concern of all men, as then God ever shows himself gracious, compassionate, and forgiving toward them in their times of need ; that this manifestation of kindness, however, on the part of God, is not confined to the Jews only, but extends equally to the Gentiles, whenever they repent and turn to the Lord." *

---

* *Das Buch Jonas*, durch Dr A. W. Krahmer, Marburg, second edition, pp. 13, 14. It is for the Jews in their relation to the Gentiles at large that the author understands the above ideas to be inculcated in the book of Jonah, and as a corrective particularly against the pharisaical notions formerly adverted to. The respectable author of the article JONAH, in Kitto's *Biblical Cyclopedia*, has somehow fallen into a mistake regarding the view of Krahmer, when he represents it as pointing specially to the relation of the Jews toward the Samaritans. Krahmer merely sup-

Now, this partial and defective exhibition of the contents of the book of Jonah is itself, as we have said, the grand reason for deserting the high-road of scriptural statement, and betaking to the by-paths of fable and conjecture. Authors set out with the assertion, that such *must* be the whole of the matter, and that hence the book must, when collateral circumstances are taken into account, have been of comparatively recent origin, and of fanciful construction. We have shown, however, that what has now been stated is not a fair or proper representation of the great object of the book—that the transactions there recorded had ends to serve far more directly, and indeed *most* directly and immediately, connected with Israel, as it stood in the very age of Jonah; and thus the whole view, with its gratuitous suppositions and slender probabilities, sinks into the condition of an arbitrary, needless, and shallow hypothesis. Like many other interpretations from the same school, it proceeds upon that superficial method of handling a subject, which hastily calls in the aid of conjecture to dispose of the difficulties that attend it, instead of seeking to clear the way to a satisfactory and well-grounded solution of them by a careful and comprehensive investigation.

But, granting for a moment that the book might

poses, that, in addition to the proper aim and direct instruction of the book, Jonah in his *person* and *origin* was designed to carry some reference to the Samaritans; but his way of making this out is quite fanciful and ridiculous.

have had such an origin, and be made up of such
fanciful materials, why should Jonah in particular, of
all the ancient prophets, have been singled out to be
the Coryphæus in a parabolical representation, which
was to convey suitable admonitions to the pharisaical
bigots of a later age? Jonah, especially, whose own
age was so palpably characterised by a spirit entirely
the reverse? This is a pinching point for the theorists; and Krahmer conceives (p. 5) that most interpreters have failed of a thorough insight into the
nature of the book, from not apprehending the exact
suitableness of Jonah to form the hero of such a
piece. How does our author himself propose to
explicate the difficulty? Thus, namely, that " the
second Jeroboam, under whom Jonah lived, as an
idolater and seducer of his subjects to idolatry, must
have appeared to persons of strong theocratical tendencies highly deserving of punishment, while still
Jehovah caused prosperity to be promised to him, and
also fulfilled what was promised, simply because the
wretchedness of his equally guilty subjects had moved
compassion in God. From which it manifestly follows, that God, in his government of the world, deals
with men, not according to their external religious
sect or profession, but according to their spiritual
condition, and that he is not solicitous of merely outward and ceremonial respect, but looks rather to the
sincere regard with which men honour the Godhead."
That is, God treats two parties in Jonah's time, *both
equally bad*, with signal marks of kindness, though

one of these thought the other deserving of very different treatment; therefore Jonah was peculiarly fit
to be chosen as the representative of an instruction
which specially taught the propriety of God's extending mercy and forgiveness to *the penitent and reformed*, though the recipients should be Gentiles and
not Jews. Admirable logic! Was there ever a more
lame and impotent conclusion? From prosperity bestowed on the wicked and undeserving, to proceed to
argue the justice of showing favour to the God-fear-
ing and penitent! And then, where is the proof, or
so much as the shadow of a proof, that such a theocratical, narrow-minded, pharisaical party existed in
Israel at Jonah's time, and murmured because they
were not alone prospered, but that Jeroboam also and
his idolatrous party shared in the prosperity? Our
author confesses there is no record of this, but inno-
cently asks, Who, in the absence of any thing to the
contrary, would venture to deny that such was the
case? and then adds, that very likely some tradition
of the kind had been handed down to succeeding
generations. What a miserable foundation for a
hypothesis that presumes to challenge our belief in
preference to the historical verity of this portion of
the word of God!

The other grounds of this baseless theory neither
require nor deserve any lengthened consideration.
Thus it is alleged as an objection that the book is
written, not in Jonah's name, but in the third person,
apparently by another hand—as if the historical por-

tions of Isaiah's prophecies, and Jeremiah's, and in great part also those of Daniel, were not in like manner written in the third person. There is, however, the prayer, in which Jonah speaks in his own person. But then this prayer is made up of portions from the Psalms, and some of these psalms composed long after the age of the historical Jonah. This ground-less allegation regarding quotations from psalms of a late period, we have already noticed in the first part of these Supplementary Remarks; and in the body of the work, when considering the prayer itself, we pointed out how natural it was for Jonah then to lean upon the recorded experiences of former saints of God. But there is no superscription to the book, we are again told, such as we usually find in the prophets, and no mention of the king's reign under which the prophecy was delivered—is not this a proof that the book was composed by a late hand, and at a time when kings no longer reigned over Israel? Strange! Why could not that imaginary late hand stamp the book with the name of a king's reign, as well as connect the transactions with the person of a prophet? And where, we ask, is the superscription at Daniel's prophecies? or where the indication of the reign under which Joel, or Nahum, or Habakkuk prophesied? Besides, the part assigned to Jonah in his book bears more resemblance to what is recorded of Elijah and Elisha than the part performed by the later prophets; and formal superscriptions or announcements such

as were wont to be placed over prophetic visions to
mark when they were given, were not to be expected
here, where outward action rather than internal vision
was the thing chiefly to be brought into view.

But the grand objection, no doubt, with the class
of authors now under consideration, is the miraculous
character of that portion of the book which records
the prophet's own history, and the special interposi-
tions of God's hand which appear throughout the
narrative. This strikes directly on the infidel tendencies, which are the real mother that gives birth to
all this species of conjectural interpretation; and the
question narrows itself to the point, whether may we
most readily hold this portion of Scripture to speak
false, or that such wonders actually took place in
the history of Jonah? That our Lord appeals to
the wonders as real facts in providence, and fitting
signs of the much more marvellous things that were
to appear in him, can admit of no doubt with any
unsophisticated and candid mind; so that the question of the credibility of the book of Jonah carries
along with it that also of Jesus Christ. The *grand*
wonder still is, that Jesus himself should have died
and risen again to immortal life as the Saviour of
sinners—a fact which lies at the foundation of all
Christianity, and which is supported by evidence the
most conclusive and irrefragable. And for any one
who admits the grand wonder to dispute and cavil
at the *minor* wonders, which not only lie enfolded

in the authority of this, but which also stand in a relation of subservience to it and necessary preparation for it, is as little consistent with sound reason as it is with an intelligent and living faith; and in proportion as true learning and vital religion flourish, it must also give way and disappear.